Copy

GCSE Home Economics

HOME AND CONSUMER

Dodie Roe

Longman

CONTENTS

Preface

This book is one of a series of four, written particularly to help teachers interpret and pupils succeed in the GCSE examination courses in Home Economics. The authors have worked together on developing a problem-solving approach and have tried ideas out in the classroom. The other books in the series are:

Families and Child Development
Textiles for People
Food for Health

What is so special about this examination?
One of the aims of the GCSE examination course is to develop the skills of decision making, which are necessary throughout life. It also aims to help individuals to lead effective lives as members of the family and community, and to provide them with the management skills to use resources wisely and to recognise the interrelationship between the need for food, clothing, shelter, and security.

What does this approach entail?
The authors of these books have used the subject matter of Home Economics to provide pupils with opportunities to:
   – identify needs in a particular area;
   – recall, seek out, and apply knowledge relevant to the situation;
   – identify ways of carrying out a task or solving a problem, isolating the priorities;
   – decide upon and plan a course of action;
   – carry out a course of action;
   – evaluate the effectiveness of the course of action.

How do these books help with this approach?
The books are written with an alphabetical sequence of topics, similar to a catalogue, not as a course to be followed through from beginning to end. Units of work from within one book, or from across several can, therefore, be put together as the teacher wishes. This supports the underlying philosophy of the GCSE course to integrate the four main aspects of Home Economics.

The topics in the catalogue start from the pupils' own knowledge, provide trigger material, practical exercises, discussion points, ideas for visits and speakers, and suggest resources to extend experience.

Home and Consumer aims to develop the pupils' skills of organisation and management of resources in the home, for example time, money, space, energy, equipment, and to foster responsibility in family relationships and as individuals and members of a community.

Dodie Roe *Series editor*

About using this book

This book will help you to make decisions in the home. As a member of a family in the home and in the community you will often be faced with making decisions, for example:

about money when deciding on priorities for spending;
about time when deciding which jobs to do first;
about space when planning a room;
about energy when trying to decide how to cut down on heating bills;
about equipment when choosing the right tools for the job;
about materials when deciding which soap powder to use;
about people when deciding who should be responsible for pets.

When faced with a decision you have to make or a task that needs doing it may help you:

1) To think about what the problem really is. Try to explain it to yourself or someone else, or write it down.

2) To find out as much as you can from other people, from books, television, videos, magazines, specialist organisations; to be aware of any laws which can help you with problems, so that you are as well prepared as possible.

3) To consider all the possible ways of carrying out the task or solving the problem.

4) To decide on your course of action and plan how to carry it out.

5) To carry out the plan of action.

6) To assess how successful your course of action has been.

Here is a very simple example:

i) Your windows are dirty. The window cleaner has left a card saying he will call next week, but the rate he is charging seems rather expensive. In the shop you have seen:
a) an aerosol window cleaner
b) a pink liquid window polish
c) a clear window polish in a refillable bottle
d) an all-purpose cleaner which says it is suitable for windows.
Problem: Should you clean the windows yourself or employ a window cleaner? If you do them yourself which window cleaner will you use?

ii) Ask other people which cleaner they use and how successful it is.
Ask if neighbours have had the window cleaner and if his results were good. Read the topic in this book on aerosols, and any other information you can find about different types of cleaners.
Collect information about the cost and weight of the cleaners you have seen in the shop.

Read the instructions on the bottles.

iii) Compare the weight and cost of the different cleaners. Find out which will be the most economical to use.

Compare the cost with what the window cleaner will charge. Have you got time to clean the windows yourself? When will you fit it in? Remember you will still have to clean the insides, even if the window cleaner cleans the outside.

Have you got a ladder or is it possible to reach the outsides of the windows from the inside?

Are there any difficult or dangerous windows which you would not be able to reach, but the window cleaner could?

If you could try out each cleaner how would you conduct a test to compare the results? Sometimes you need to try out different makes over a period of time to find out which suits you best.

iv) You decide you can find the time to clean the windows by preparing a meal the day before to cook in the oven while you do it. You choose the liquid, pink window cleaner, because you get more for your money, the spray polish may go all over the curtains, it may not be as easy to see the clear polish when cleaning it off, and the all-purpose cleaner is the most expensive.

v) You clean the windows, following the instructions on the bottle, and time how long it takes.

vi) It takes you longer than you think to clean all the windows, but the results are good – no corners with polish left in. It has only cost you a fraction of the window cleaner's cost and you still have some cleaner left for another time. You think about how often they will need doing and decide it is probably worth re-arranging jobs now and again, or having a quick meal for a change. Perhaps next time younger members of the family could be encouraged to help.

These are your decisions pages. You should be able to use the same decision making process for other occasions.

There is a grey line down the outside edges of these pages so that you can pick them out easily.

There are three symbols used in this book:

 means that you have to "collect" something.

 means that you have to "send for" something.

 means that you can find out more information by looking either in another part of this book; or in another book in this series; or in a computer program, leaflet, booklet, or other publication; or by visiting somewhere or asking someone to visit you.

Adhesives

Figure 1   Some of the many adhesives available today.

Adhesives are used to fix (glue) two surfaces together.

   You have probably mended something yourself in this way, only to find that it comes unstuck again in a short time. Or you may have bought something which came apart because the glue wasn't strong enough. The only way to find out about adhesives in detail is to read the small print on the back of the pack. If you look in the adhesives department of your local do-it-yourself shop you will probably see a vast range of adhesives; these can be used for all sorts of jobs around the home.

   How do you know which one to choose?

   Your choice will depend on the type of materials to be stuck together, whether you need the job done quickly or not, and how long you expect it to last.

Type of adhesive	Colour		Use for
Cellulose adhesives	Clear	Suitable for glass and china. Not strong, but quick setting. Remove with nail varnish remover.	Glass, china, model-making
Contact adhesives	Brown	These adhesives have to be spread on both surfaces, then left for about 15 minutes before joining. They make a very permanent join. They contain solvents, *e.g.* petroleum spirit. It is dangerous to breathe these solvents. See page 5. Not suitable for polystyrene. Remove with nail varnish remover or special cleaner.	Formica, rubber, wood, hardboard, plastics and most other surfaces
Clear glue	Clear	Sticks most surfaces, immediately.	Paper, fabric, leather, wood, PVC, etc.
Cyanoacrylates (superglues)	Clear	Superglues stick things together in seconds, using only a few drops, so they are good for quick repair jobs. They are not suitable for anything which will be washed in hot water. Because they are so quick it is very easy to stick your fingers together or stick to anything you touch. See page 5. Remove immediately with hot water.	Metal, rubber, jewellery, wood
Epoxy resins	Cream or brown	These adhesives are sold in two tubes containing different chemicals, one of which is a hardener. When the contents of the two tubes are mixed together in the right quantities a firm seal is made, which sets hard in about 24 hours. They will stick almost anything very firmly, but are expensive for large jobs. Remove immediately with methylated spirit.	Glass, china, anything which needs washing, most other surfaces

Type of adhesive	Colour		Use for
Gums, pastes	White or clear	Comes as a powder (*e.g.* wallpaper paste), in a bottle, or easily used gluestick. Remove with water.	Paper, cardboard
PVA adhesives	White	Suitable for wood, which is best clamped together while drying. These adhesives set in 20 minutes and dry completely in 24 hours. Remove with water.	Wood
PVC adhesives	Clear	Suitable for plastic joins, but can cause some plastics to wrinkle.	Plastic rainwear, bags, car seat covers
Spray glue	Clear	This is adhesive which comes in an aerosol spray. It gives a very flat join for photographs or paper, and it is possible to peel things off a few times until they are in the right place. It is expensive compared with other glues which are suitable for paper, but gives a good finish.	Paper, card
Tile adhesives	White or brown	There are special adhesives available for sticking wood, ceramics, and polystyrene, and carpet tiles. You will need to consider whether the adhesive needs to be waterproof, *e.g.* for use in a bathroom.	Ceramic, polystyrene, and carpet tiles

There are several different types of adhesive. There is a summary of them in the table on pages 2 and 3.

You will probably not find these adhesives being sold under these names. They will be sold under trade names such as Bostik or Araldite.

Activities

Make a survey of the different types of adhesives in your local do-it-yourself shop, or get everyone in the group to bring in the ones they have at home. Read the small print on the packet and make a note of the weight and cost.

Using the information in the table on pages 2 and 3, and on the adhesive containers you have, make a chart to help you to choose the right adhesive for the job.

Make your chart under the following headings:

Type of adhesive
Trade name
Suitable for
Not suitable for
Weight
Cost
Safety warnings given on container

How many of the adhesives do the same job? Which gives the most for your money?

Think up a consumer test to see which would be the best adhesive for sticking:
photographs on to a poster
carpet tiles to the floor.

Describe how you would carry out the test and record the results. How would you decide how successful the test had been?

Make a list of the adhesives you think it would be useful to keep in the home for emergencies.

Which adhesives would you use for the mending jobs in figure 2?

 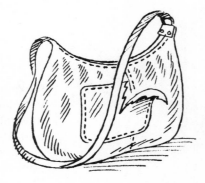

Figure 2   (part)

Figure 2 (continued)

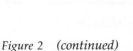

Safety with adhesives

Many adhesives give off fumes. If these are breathed it may make you feel sick, dizzy, or faint. Breathing these fumes repeatedly can be addictive (you can't stop). The fumes may damage the liver and kidneys and can lead to death. This is why the sale of adhesives is restricted in some shops.

These fumes are also flammable (easily set on fire), so adhesives should be used out of doors when possible or in a well-ventilated room (open all the windows).

Some adhesives can cause skin irritation so wash splashes off with water immediately.

When using quick-drying adhesives like superglue it is easy for fingers to become stuck to each other or to something else. If this happens peel apart using hot soapy water and a blunt edge (*e.g.* the handle of a teaspoon). If eyelids become stuck together bathe them with lots of water. *Don't panic*. If you do not succeed in separating fingers or eyelids the hospital will, so seek help.

Some wallpaper pastes contain fungicides to help stop mould growing on the walls. Wash hands after using wallpaper pastes to stop contamination spreading.

Advertising

Collect advertisements from different newspapers or magazines for different products.

Advertising is a way in which those who have a product or service to sell can tell their customers about it.

This may be done by:

television or cinema commercials;
advertisements in newspapers or magazines;
posters or billboards;
display cards;
free samples and trial offers;
carrier bags;
T-shirts.

Advertising can sometimes help to cut the cost of things. Newspapers and magazines would be much more expensive if they had no advertisements. But other things, *e.g.* food, may be a little more expensive (about 2%) to cover the cost of advertising.

Activities

Look at the advertisements you have collected.
OR
Choose one product, *e.g.* breakfast cereals, washing powder. Watch the television commercials for these products over a week.

For each advertisement ask the following questions:

1) What information does the advertisement give about the product? Did it tell you where to buy it?

2) Was it easy to understand? An advertisement which is too long or complicated will not be read.

Compare the advertisement for soap which was used in 1889 (figure 3) with the advertisement for eggs used in 1985 (figure 4). Which is the most effective?

See if you can find examples of other advertisements from the past in books. Would they be suitable today?

3) Were words like *fresh, cool, golden* and *natural* repeated often?

What other examples of words like this can you find? These words make us feel that a product must be good (they appeal to our emotions). Which words did you notice? Often the words

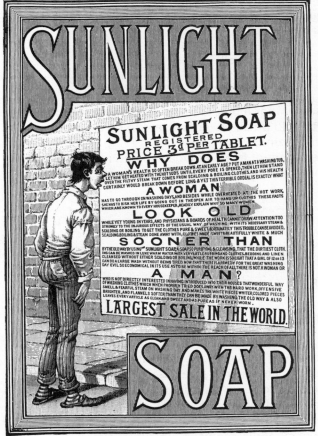

Figure 3

"He's all mixed up but I love him"

Go smash an egg

Figure 4

"probably", "most", "generally" or other similar words will be used to prevent an advertisement from being untrue.

Were any catchy phrases or slogans used like "nothing acts faster . . .", "drinka pinta milka day"?.

4) Was music used and did it make any difference to the success of the advertisement?

5) Does the advertisement use a "stereotype", for example women happily cleaning the house, the family sitting down together to meals, or a glamorous figure like the dashing airline pilot? These stereotypes are used to persuade you that you could become like the person if only you used the product. Who is the advertisement aimed at: housewife, car owner, teenager, child, etc.?

6) Are advertisements for children's toys or sweets shown on television at times when children will be watching? What sort of magazines do advertisements like this appear in? Where would you

expect to find advertisements for cars and fast food?

Arrange your advertisements in order of success. Discuss the reasons for your order.

Design an advertisement for a pair of jeans, remembering the points you made above. It could be an advertisement to be shown on television or for a magazine.

Choose one advertisement from a magazine and make a poster showing other people what to look for when reading advertisements.

Can we be protected from advertisements making claims which are untrue?

1) Legal controls

There are about fifty Acts of Parliament which affect advertising, *e.g.* the Trade Descriptions Act (TDA) makes it an offence for anyone to give a false description of goods or to give false or misleading information. However, words like "amazing value" or "virtually unbeatable" are not covered by the law as they cannot be proved or disproved. "Misleading" information is difficult to prove. The Race Relations Act prevents racial discrimination in advertising.

Television commercials are controlled by the Independent Broadcasting Authority (IBA) Act. The IBA sells time to advertisers and this provides the money for producing programmes. The Act states that advertising must be at the beginning or end of programmes, or in a natural break, so that it is clear that the programme has stopped and the advertisement begun. There is a limit to the time advertisements may be shown. They cannot be shown during school broadcasts, religious programmes, or royal occasions, and they may not be religious or political or include swearing or violence. Cigarettes and betting cannot be advertised, and alcoholic drink advertisements must not make it look as if drink leads to success or gain. All advertisements have to be seen by the IBA Advertising Control Officer before they are broadcast and about 20% are turned down.

2) Voluntary controls

These controls are not law, but are followed by advertisers. The British Code of Advertising Practice (BCAP) says that all advertising should be "legal, decent, honest, and truthful". It lays down guidelines for the advertising of products, which advertisers are encouraged to follow. The code also applies to mail order advertisements, other than those in the catalogues of major mail order firms. The largest catalogue sales firms belong to the Mail Order Traders Association.

The Advertising Standards Authority (ASA), address on page 180, makes sure the guidelines are followed. If you think that an advertisement is misleading, inaccurate, or offensive you can write to the ASA who will investigate the complaint. They also produce a useful wall chart.

SEE ALSO

Consumer protection for more information about your rights when buying goods or services.
Shopping for information about other influences when buying.
The Advertising Standards Authority (ASA) produces a wall chart (address on page 180).

Aerosols

Figure 5 A selection of aerosol products.

Activities

Look around your own home and make a list of all the things which are sold in aerosol sprays. The kitchen, bathroom, bedroom, or garden shed are all good starting points.

Choose one of your products and answer the following questions about it.

Can the product be bought in other ways, *e.g.* as liquid in a bottle?

Will it harm any surfaces?

How much does it contain?

How much does it cost? Compare with buying a similar product in other containers.

Is it easier to use, *e.g.* spray polish may not need such hard rubbing?

How long would you expect it to last?

Does it smell pleasant?

Is there any warning about getting rid of the can, or using it in certain places?

Try using the product following the instructions exactly as on the container. Is this how you always use it?

Use a spray shoe cleaner with the shoe placed on a sheet of coloured paper (figure 6). Notice how much of the spray goes on the paper. Is this an economical way of buying shoe polish?

Figure 6 Using spray shoe cleaner.

What kind of test could you devise for testing the efficiency of deodorants, furniture polish, or fresh air sprays? How would you record your results?

Aerosols can be harmful

A lot of the aerosol spray just gets wasted into the air. Some of the chemicals used to propel (spray) the contents of an aerosol are damaging the ozone layer around the Earth. This is the layer of the Earth's atmosphere which protects us from the harmful effects of the Sun's rays.

Aerosols can be dangerous

Don't spray aerosols near food. They can be poisonous.

Always spray away from the face to avoid damage to eyes.

Never throw aerosols on to the fire, even when empty. They are pressurised and can explode.

Never let children play with aerosol sprays. Not long ago a small child died from breathing the fumes from a hair spray which he had taken off the shelf, while bathing.

Read the instructions carefully. Some sprays can damage some surfaces.

Assurance

Assurance is a way of providing for an event which you know is going to happen one day – in the case opposite, death. It is a way of making sure the people who depend on you are provided for. Sometimes you can cash in the policy after a set time. How long is this term in figure 7?

Activity

How can you be sure that this is a wise way to spend your money?
   In figure 7 Steve is paying out £20 a month for 10 years. How much will he have paid in this time?

£20 (amount per month) × 12 (months) × 10 (years)
= £ . . . (amount paid after 10 years)

   How much is he promised in the advertisement?
   When Steve pays in his £20 a month this money is invested by the Assurance Company. He will only get the amount shown if the company's trust fund, in which the money is invested, goes on growing at the rate of 14.1 per cent. In the very small print you will find out how much Steve will get if the rate is only 8 per cent. How much will this be? Look again at how much he has paid in.
   Would Steve have been better off putting his £20 in the Building Society? If the interest rate in the Building Society were 8 per cent the amount of money he would have after six months would be:

£120 (amount Steve pays over 6 months) $+\left(120 \times \dfrac{8}{100} \times \dfrac{1}{2}\right)$

He might get a better rate of interest for saving over a long time, and in the next six months he would also get interest on the interest. What would Steve not have if he spent his money in this way?

Working out whether assurance is worth while is not easy but try to remember to do four things:
*Read the small print.
*Work out exactly how much you will be paying.
*Compare this with other ways of saving.
*Don't be tempted by bribes. What is offered in figure 7?

SEE ALSO

Insurance for how to protect yourself against things which *might* happen.
Savings for more about ways of saving money.

Fill in the coupon to-day! And get your **FREE** calculator.

NAME ....

ADDRESS...

....

AGE.................. OCCUPATION.............................

Figure 7

This advertisement covers only the basic details of our policy. For full information, complete and return the coupon. There's no obligation.

The examples quoted apply to a 25-year-old man contributing £20 per month. They are based on an average annual growth rate of 14.1% recorded over the last 10 years in the Norton Life Growth Fund.

Future values cannot be guaranteed and can fall as well as rise. As a guide, the following illustration is based on a growth rate of only 8% per annum which is conservative compared with past performance. A man aged 25 contributing £20 per month would have life cover of £53,423 at age 65, a tax-free cash value of £1,879 after 10 years, and £27,132 at age 65.

Budgeting

Collect leaflets about the services offered from banks and the Girobank.
Send for *Understanding banking* and sample bank cards from the Banking Information Service (address on page 180).

When you receive money as earnings, dole money, pocket money, etc., you have to make a number of decisions about how to spend it. What you *want* to spend and what you *can* spend are often very different. If you can't afford everything you want, then you have to decide which things are most important to you. You have to assess your priorities.

Here is a list of some of the things you might spend money on at some time of your life:

rent for home*	savings*
rates*	holidays
mortgage*	gardening
money to family for living at home	pets
credit repayments for goods bought*	repairs to appliances
fuel, *e.g.* gas, electricity, oil, coal*	cleaning
food	car, motor bike
clothes	make-up
fares	pocket money
entertainment	telephone charges
newspapers, magazines	television licence
insurance*, assurance*	rent, *e.g.* for television

If you do not understand the meaning of the items which are starred there is a section about them in the book to which you can refer.

Activity

From the list above write down your priorities for spending the money you have regularly. If your money was cut, suddenly, by half, what items could you cut down or do without?

What might the priorities be for:

someone living in a bed-sitter, working in a travel agent's in a town six miles away;
someone on the dole, living at home with parents;
someone working at Marks and Spencer who has a free uniform and subsidised meals;

someone who is a student living in a nurse's home;
someone who is a YTS student living with Dad?

What do you think would be covered by "pocket money" or
"entertainment"? Where will the money for soap and other cleaning
agents come from?

When you are working out your priorities for spending there are some
fixed expenses for which you should set aside money first, for example
rent or mortgage, rates, tax, credit repayments. Working out how
much you will have left to spend on yourself after all the essential bills
are paid is called "budgeting".

It is easiest to work out a budget for the period over which you are
paid. If you are paid weekly, work out a weekly budget. Some bills,
like gas or electricity, come once a quarter (3 monthly) so you will need
to put some money by each week for this. Other bills, like the
television licence, come yearly, so money must be put by for this, or
you might decide to buy stamps towards the licence each week.

To draw up a budget you will need to rule out rows and columns as
in figure 8.

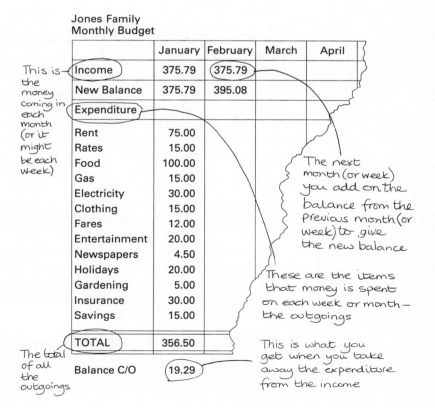

Jones Family
Monthly Budget

	January	February	March	April
Income	375.79	375.79		
New Balance	375.79	395.08		
Expenditure				
Rent	75.00			
Rates	15.00			
Food	100.00			
Gas	15.00			
Electricity	30.00			
Clothing	15.00			
Fares	12.00			
Entertainment	20.00			
Newspapers	4.50			
Holidays	20.00			
Gardening	5.00			
Insurance	30.00			
Savings	15.00			
TOTAL	356.50			
Balance C/O	19.29			

This is the money coming in each month (or it might be each week)

The next month (or week) you add on the balance from the previous month (or week) to give the new balance

These are the items that money is spent on each week or month — the outgoings

This is what you get when you take away the expenditure from the income

The total of all the outgoings

Figure 8   This budget has been worked out monthly.

Draw up a simple budget for your own weekly spending in the same way.

A calculator is useful when working out a budget, or you could use a "spreadsheet" program on the computer to do the calculations for you.

Here is a general guide to the percentage of your income you might expect to spend weekly when running a home of your own.

Rent or mortgage, rates, tax	25 per cent
Food	30 per cent
Fuel	10 per cent
Clothes	10 per cent
Household expenses (cleaning, detergents, etc.)	5 per cent
Regular savings, holidays, television	10 per cent
Pocket money	5 per cent
Elasticity (so that the budget will not be too tightly planned)	5 per cent

The amount for "elasticity" is important in case you have any unexpected bills, or for times like Christmas which can be more expensive.

Discussion

When you go out for a meal or to the cinema with a girl/boy friend should you each pay half towards the evening?

Adults who are not earning money of their own from a job should receive an "allowance" for themselves, from their partner.

How will giving young children "pocket money" help them to learn to manage money wisely? Should they receive pocket money in return for jobs done?

Managing money – bank accounts

You may find it useful to open a bank account when you start to receive regular sums of money as wages, YTS earnings, or as a student grant. This money can be paid directly into the bank for you.

The "big four" banks are Midland, Lloyds, Barclays, and National Westminster, but there are others.

Activity

Make a list of the banks in your own area.

You can go into any branch of a bank to open an account with an amount as small as a pound. The kind of account which enables you to take money in and out is called a current account. To pay money in you fill in a slip from the back of the cheque book or from the bank counter, and hand it in with the money. To take money out you write yourself a cheque. You can also pay for goods or services by cheque.

The bank will send you a list of the transactions you have made every three months, or more often if you ask for it. It is probably a good idea to have a statement at least once a month to keep check of your spending.

It is also possible to open a deposit account for saving money which builds up interest. This type of account does not have a cheque book.

Banks can also help you to budget. With a budget account you can add up all your bills for a year, divide this amount by twelve and pay this amount into the bank monthly. As your bills come in and you pay them by cheque, the bank will pay out the money for you even if you haven't got enough in the bank at the right time, because they know you will have paid in enough money to cover all the bills by the end of the year.

You can also have an account with the National Girobank, operated by the Post Office. The Girobank has current and deposit accounts, but you are limited to two post offices where you can draw money, unless you make special arrangements. The Girobank sends you a statement after every ten transactions.

Activity

Make a list of the advantages and disadvantages of having a bank account or a Girobank account. Use the leaflets you have collected to help you.

SEE ALSO

Assurance
Credit
Fuel
Insurance   for more information about fixed outgoings
Mortgages   from your income.
Paying for goods
Rates
Savings

QUICKCALC Spreadsheet program for the BBC computer available from Beebugsoft (address on page 180).
Multiplan Spreadsheet program for the RML380/480Z from RML (address on page 180).

Cleaning

Keeping a home clean will make it a more pleasant and healthy place to be for all the members of the family.

Organising the cleaning of a home efficiently will mean that everyone has more time for interests and hobbies.

Activity

Put these jobs into three lists:
1) to be done every day
2) to be done once a week
3) to be done less frequently, for example at spring cleaning time.

Dusting
Shampooing carpets
Cleaning the toilet
Opening windows to air rooms
Cleaning out food cupboards
Vacuum cleaning carpets
Washing down paintwork
Defrosting the refrigerator
Emptying ash trays/waste bins
Making beds
Cleaning windows
Cleaning the bath
Polishing wooden surfaces
Cleaning the cooker
Cleaning the wash basins
Cleaning sinks, draining boards

Who does the cleaning?

It is usually the person who spends the most time in the home who does the cleaning. But if all partners in a home are out at work jobs need to be shared, so that everyone has time for some leisure.

Discussion

How do you think jobs could be shared?

If there are children they can be encouraged to help too. Which jobs in the home would you expect everyone to do for themselves?

Cleaning equipment

Having the right tools and cleaning agents makes it easier to do the cleaning well.

Activity

Make a list of cleaning equipment you would need for jobs listed on page 18.

Many of the cleaning agents available can do more than one job. Some of the things to think of when buying cleaning agents are:
1) What it can be used for.
2) Cost.
3) How long you expect it to last.
4) How it should be used – does it need a lot of hard rubbing, for example.
5) Does it have a pleasant smell?
6) Can it harm any surfaces?

Activity

Choose a range of furniture polishes, surface cleaners, carpet shampoos, or other cleaning agents. Think up a consumer test to find out which would be the best for the job. How would you assess the results of your test? Make a chart to display the results.

SEE ALSO

Aerosols for more about cleaning agents.
Budgeting for more about cleaning costs.
Equipment for more about cleaning equipment.

Colour schemes

 Collect wallpaper books, scraps of furnishing fabrics and floor coverings, paint charts.

Red, yellow, and blue are the **primary** colours, from which all other colours are made.

By mixing two primary colours together we get the **complementary** colours. For example, by mixing red and yellow we get orange.

Activity

Make a copy of the colour wheel (see the colour section, between pages 106 and 107) and fill in orange in section 1. Fill in sections 2 and 3 with the other colours made by mixing primary colours together.

If you use all the primary colours together in a room the effect can be dazzling! So, often we choose one colour, then pick others which contrast or tone with it.

To find the strongest possible contrast for a colour look at its opposite in the colour wheel. For example, the strongest contrast for yellow would be purple.

What would the strongest contrast for orange be? And for green?

Colours which tone are colours which are near each other in the colour wheel. For example, all the shades of blue from turquoise (a green/blue) through to purple (a red/blue). Some colours are warmer in feel, for example reds, yellows, and oranges; others are colder, for example blues and greens. Warm colours can be used to make a cold (north-facing) room appear warmer. Cold colours can be used to create a cool colour scheme.

Activity

Using scraps of wallpaper or fabric, or paint charts show the tones which might come between red and yellow or between yellow and green.

Texture is the way things feel when you rub your hand over them. It helps to make a home interesting as well as colour. Imagine a home where the wall, floor, and ceiling all looked the same!

Activities

Find three materials of the same texture, but different colours.
Now find three materials of different texture, but the same colour.

Plan a colour scheme for your own room, showing what colours and textures you have used for wall/floor/window coverings, cushions, etc. Draw a plan of your room and use samples of fabric, paint, wallpaper, and floor coverings to illustrate your choice.

SEE ALSO
Furnishings for more about choosing soft furnishings for the home.

Consumer information

Collect copies of *Which?* magazine.
Send for the leaflet "Taking the lid off testing" from the
Education Department, British Standards Institution (address on
page 180).

We sometimes need expert help when we have a problem – someone
to talk the problem over with, or a book, leaflet, or article so that we
can read about another point of view. It often helps to talk to several
people, or read articles written by more than one person before making
up your own mind.

If you have problems about buying goods or services there are
several places you can go for help and the main ones are listed below.

Activity

You might be able to ask some of these people to speak to your
class about their jobs. You can find many of their addresses in your
local library, in the telephone directory, or in a local newspaper. If
this is possible make a list of questions you would like to ask before
the talk, for example . . . where to go for advice? . . . what kind of
advice? . . . when is legal help necessary? . . . does advice cost
money? . . . etc.

You could then arrange a display of "Consumer advice in my
town" for the rest of the school.

Where to go for help

1 The Trading Standards Department

This department will help if you have been wrongly charged or the
description on something you bought is misleading, for example it
checks the accuracy of petrol pumps at filling stations.

It also keeps an eye on safety, for example it watches out for
dangerous toys.

It also investigates complaints about food and labelling, for example
it checks that food is the correct weight and the contents are accurately
described.

And it checks the licences of traders offering credit.

The Trading Standards Department is usually found in the town or county hall.

2 Environmental Health Departments

These will help if you have a problem about, for example, dirty plates in a restaurant or dirty towels in a hairdressing salon – things which affect health.

The Environmental Health Department is usually found in the town or county hall.

3 Citizens Advice Bureaux

These will help with any enquiries about law, money matters, health, housing, goods, or services. They will either help you themselves, or put you in touch with the right person.

4 Consumer Advice Centres

These will help with anything from planning a large purchase or dealing with a bad buy, with money or legal problems, to making a will.

Consumer Advice Centres are usually in shopping centres.

Where to look for help

1 *Which?*

Which? is a magazine published by the Consumers' Association. The Consumers' Association tests things like washing machines, face creams, and holidays, and gives a report and the "best buy" in the *Which?* magazine.

Activities

Read about the tests carried out, and how a "best buy" is decided, in your copies of *Which?* magazine.

Design your own *Which?* test for an electric kettle. You will need to test a number of different kettles, like those in figure 9.

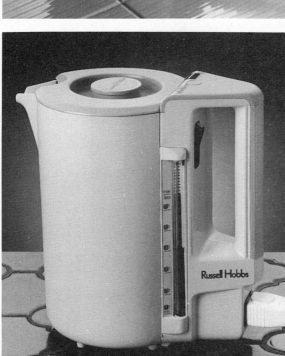

Figure 9   Range of electric kettles.

2 The Office of Fair Trading

This department publishes information to help people to know about their rights as a shopper, for instance the "codes of practice" for buying items such as electrical goods, cars, furniture, funerals, package holidays, etc.

The address of the Office of Fair Trading is given on page 180.

3 The British Standards Institution

This organisation tests a wide variety of goods sent to them by the manufacturers. The goods are measured, bounced, bumped, set on fire, left out in the rain, dropped from great heights, and put through a range of other tests to check that they are up to scratch, safe, and hard-wearing. If the goods pass all the tests they are awarded the BSI Kitemark.

The address of the British Standards Institution is given on page 180.

Discussion

What sort of testing do you think a child's teddy bear might have? Figure 10 may help you to think about the tests.

Figure 10

SEE ALSO

Consumer protection for help if things go wrong, and for a list of leaflets available from the Office of Fair Trading.
Shopping for information about buying goods, and for a list of leaflets available from the Office of Fair Trading.
Labelling for labels to look for on goods, and for more about the BSI Kitemark.

See the book *Families and Child Development* (in this series) for more on the choice and safety of children's toys.

Consumer protection

Send for the following items, which are all available from the Office of Fair Trading (address on page 180).

Free booklets: "How to put things right", "I'm going to take it further.".

Free posters: Car problems, Receipts, Faulty footwear, Buying in sales.

Videos/Tape slides (available on hire): "Dog days" (looks at the Sale of Goods Act), "A dog deceived" (looks at the Trade Descriptions Act), "You must be joking grandma" (looks at the Supply of Goods and Services Act – not applicable in Scotland). (These are also available for sale, together.)

Discussion

Have you or your friends or parents ever had any problems with goods or services that they have bought?

Look at the examples in figure 11, below and on the next page.

Goods

Services

Figure 11   (part)

Goods

Figure 11   (continued)   **Services**

Write down whose fault it might have been and why. Compare your answers. Who was in the wrong? Did you read the small print in the holiday brochure? Did you read the date stamp on the biscuits? Did you keep them a month before eating? Did you look at the dry cleaning label on the skirt?

If things do go wrong, when you're buying something, there are several laws, described here, which can help to protect you. These are Acts of Parliament: discuss how they relate to any of the problems above.

The Sale of Goods Act (1979)

This covers the sale of all goods (including food) from shops, markets, mail order, and doorstep salesmen. When you offer to buy something you enter into a contract which means that:

1) The goods must be of "merchantable quality". This means they must be reasonably fit for the purpose for which they were bought, bearing in mind how they were described and the cost.

2) The goods must be fit for their purpose, *e.g.* a lawn mower must mow the lawn.

3) The goods must be as described.

The Trade Descriptions Act (1968 and 1972)

This makes it a criminal offence for traders to describe their goods falsely.

The Weights and Measures Act (1963 and 1979)

Under this act it is an offence if the quantity (weight or volume) is not marked on packaged grocery items. (There are some exceptions – can you think what they are?) It is also an offence if the weight or quantity is not correct.

The Food and Drugs Act (1955)

The Food and Drugs Act makes it a criminal offence to sell food which is not fit to eat. Regulations cover hygiene and labelling. It is also illegal for a trader to add anything to a food which might be harmful.

The Prices Act (1974)

This act enables the government to require prices to be displayed and to control the way they are displayed. Shops must mark prices for all items of food and drink except where sold by counter service. Foods which are sold by weight such as meat, fruit, and vegetables must have the unit weight displayed, *e.g.* the price per pound or kilo. Pubs, cafés, and restaurants must display a selection of prices for meals and drinks. Garages must display the price of petrol on the pump.

The Consumer Safety Act (1978)

This makes sure that goods are labelled with warning symbols, instructions for use, or a list of ingredients to make sure that they are used correctly. It also allows the Secretary of State for Trade to step in quickly to stop the sales of dangerous goods, *e.g.* ornamental glitter lamps have been banned because they contain dangerous chemicals.

The Unsolicited Goods and Services Act (1971)

Under this act traders can be fined if they demand payments for goods they know you haven't ordered. If you receive a bill for goods you didn't order take it to your Trading Standards Officer. If you are sent goods in this way they do become your property after six months if the trader does not collect them back *or* if you write to the sender, giving your name and address and saying that the goods were "unsolicited." In this case they become yours if they are not collected within thirty days.

Activities

Find out more about these acts and examples of how they work by watching the Office of Fair Trading videos and reading "How to put things right".

If you feel you have a complaint to make about goods or services it helps to know how to complain.

Read up about this in "How to put things right". What are the three things you must do as soon as you think you have a complaint?

Write a letter of complaint to:

1) A boutique when the shirt you have bought shrinks five centimetres when you first wash it.

2) The Environmental Health Officer when you find a rusty nail in a loaf of bread.

3) The managing director of a chain store where the assistant has refused to exchange a lawn mower which doesn't work.

4) The manager of a shop which sold you an alarm clock with a six month guarantee, when the alarm stopped working after three months.

5) A mail order firm when you receive a radio which you haven't ordered.

Divide into groups and act out the following stories, letting the rest of the group give their opinions.

1) You buy a pair of shoes. The first time you wear them a heel breaks. You take them back to the shop and complain to the assistant. He isn't very happy about it, but does agree to change them for another pair. However, he finds he only has one pair left, of a different colour. You don't like these and ask for the money back. The assistant refuses, saying he has offered you another pair and you should have taken them. You take the shoes, but never wear them because you don't like the colour.

Was the assistant right?

2) You buy a video recorder which doesn't work when you get it home. You ring up the shop to complain. They say it was the manufacturer's fault and you will have to write direct to them. You refuse, saying that it was the shop's responsibility.

Who is right?

3) You see a pair of trousers you like. You try them on and they fit perfectly so you buy them. When you get home you decide the colour doesn't really go with the sweater you bought them for.

If you take them back will you be entitled to a) a refund b) an exchange c) nothing at all?

4) You buy some garden furniture from a local garden centre. The display shows a table, four chairs, and a sun umbrella and is marked "special offer". When the set is delivered the umbrella is missing. You return to the shop to complain but they explain that the umbrella was just for display and was not included in the price.

Who is at fault?

5) You see a blue tricycle in the window of a shop, which is just what your little boy wants for Christmas. When you go inside you can't find one of the same colour so you ask for the one out of the window. The assistant says "No, I'm not changing the windows until after Christmas". You say "But if it's in the window you have to sell it to me".

Which of you is right?

6) You send for a set of sheets by mail order, but when they arrive they are not the colour you ask for. You send them back and a letter asking for your money back and the postage you have had to pay.

Can you do this?

SEE ALSO

Consumer information for more about the people who can help when things go wrong (*e.g.* the Environmental Health Officer). *Shopping* for more about buying goods.

Invite your local Trading Standards Officer in to talk about the complaints he/she deals with.

Cookers

Figure 12   (part)

Figure 12 (continued)

 Collect leaflets about gas, electric, and solid fuel cookers. Send for the electrical equipment data files (see page 35).

Cookers may be gas, electric, or solid fuel, and there are a few wood-burning stoves available. When choosing what fuel to use, you will need to take into account the fuels used for other needs in a home, for example water and room heating.

If enough electricity is used, for example, you may find it economical to use cheaper off-peak electricity, but if water is heated by gas it may be more economical to use gas for cooking. Solid fuel stoves can be used to warm a kitchen as well, and are ideal if you do a lot of baking or long slow cooking.

Activities

You may be able to compare cooking costs using a computer program such as "Watts in your home" (see page 35). Choose something you can cook by different methods such as potatoes, and time the different cooking methods. Use the computer program to compare costs and prepare a block graph to show the results of your experiment.

List these points in order of importance for choosing your first cooker:

Easy to clean
Automatic timer
BEAB safety label
Can be built in or pushed into position under a work-top (slip-in)
Has economy features, *e.g.* dual rings, high-speed grill
Fan oven for more even cooking
Clock
Glass oven door
More than two shelves in the main oven
Eye-level controls
Light in main oven
Simmer rings
Two ovens
Eye-level grill
Ceramic hob
Coloured finish

Which of the cookers in your leaflets would provide you with the top 10 from your list?

If you were choosing a cooker for someone with two young children how would your list be different?

If you have a copy of "QUEST" and the electrical equipment data files (see page 35) you will be able to find out which electric cookers match your priorities for choice.

Much electrical equipment today has microelectronic controls. This means that the equipment is controlled by micro-chips instead of by clockwork or motorised parts. This may be for more accurate timing, for example in a digital clock, or because it is more convenient, for example touch controls.

Activities

List the uses of microelectronics in the cookers you have leaflets for. By the side of each write down how you think microtechnology is being used to advantage.

Choose one cooker which you think is a good example of a cooker which is safe to use. Draw a sketch of it pointing out the safety features. Do the same for a cooker which would be economical to run.

SEE ALSO

Electricity
Gas } for more about different types of fuel.
Fuel
Energy saving for ideas on how to save energy in the home.

"QUEST" and the electrical equipment data files for the BBC or RML computer, available from the Advisory Unit on Computer-Based Education (address on page 180).
"Watts in your home" computer program for the BBC or RML computer, available from Cambridge University Press (address on page 180).

Credit

Send for copies of the booklets *Shop around for credit* and *No credit* from the Office of Fair Trading (address on page 180). There is also an accompanying poster set.

When you buy something "on credit", you pay for it over a period of time.

Discussion

What sort of things do you think people buy on credit and why?

Buying things on credit is fine as long as you don't sign up to pay more than you can afford. There is more to know about credit than that, though. Some of the best places to find information about buying goods or your rights as a shopper are the local Citizens Advice Bureau, the Trading Standards Department, the Consumer Protection Department, or the Consumer Advice Centre. They will be able to give you advice and will also have leaflets like those supplied for this work. You could also send for the leaflets yourself by writing to the Office of Fair Trading (address on page 180).

Activity

Read the booklet *Shop around for credit*. This will tell you about the different ways of buying on credit and how the law protects you when making a purchase in this way. Then try the activities suggested.

You can compare the different types of credit by looking at the APR (short for annual percentage rate). This is the cost of borrowing worked out as a yearly percentage.

Activities

What are the advantages of showing the APR on goods? Collect some examples of the APR quoted in newspaper advertisements, on posters in stores, in newsagent's windows, on handbills delivered through the door, etc.

Figure 13

Choose an item, *e.g.* stereo, motor bike, washing machine (figure 13). Compare the different methods of paying for it, *e.g.* H.P., Access, Barclaycard, bank loan. Which is the cheapest method of buying?

N.B. You will need to know the current interest rates. You can find these on the money pages of some newspapers, on a Barclaycard or Access statement.

Draw up a list of rules you would give someone for buying on credit.

What are credit reference agencies? How do they collect information about people? Do you think that credit reference agencies are a good idea?

Explain the meaning of the following words:
instalment
purchase
interest
deposit
borrow
cash price.

A washing machine costs £300 if you pay cash. You have to pay a 20 per cent deposit and twelve monthly instalments of £24.20. How much credit are you paying? Fill in the blanks in the calculations below to find out.
To find out the deposit:

$$\frac{20}{100} \times £300 = £ \qquad \text{(deposit)}$$

To find out the total credit cost:

£24.20 (monthly payments) × 12 (number of instalments) =
£   + £   (deposit) = £   (total credit cost)

To find out the extra cost of credit:

£   (total credit price) − £300 (cash price) = £   (credit cost)

The Consumer Credit Act of 1974 controls credit agreements. (See the booklet *Shop around for credit* mentioned on page 36). How will the act help you if:
1) goods you've bought on credit go wrong;

2) someone stops you in the street or knocks on your door, and tries to talk you into a loan;

3) someone turns you down for credit;

4) you think your credit charges are too high;

5) you sign an H.P. agreement on the doorstep and change your mind a few hours later.

SEE ALSO

Consumer protection for information about your rights as a shopper.

Electricity

Collect fuse wire and a mains fuse, plug, flex, and assorted plug fuses.

Newspaper articles relating to accidents with electricity.

Send for the booklet *Understanding your electricity bill* from the Electricity Council (address on page 180).

Figure 14   (part)

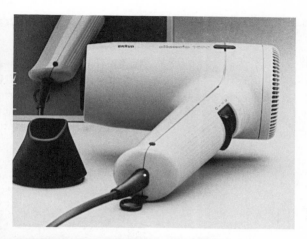

Figure 14
(continued)

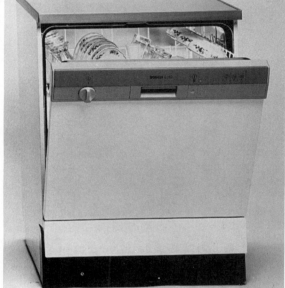

We all tend to take electricity for granted.

Activity

How do you manage without electric lights (remember the last power cuts)? What safety hazards can this create?

How would you clean carpets without an electric cleaner? How much longer would it take?

How would you keep foods fresh without a refrigerator?

Make a list of all the electrical appliances you have in your own home. Divide the list into those that are most important to you and those you could do without.

You probably made quite a long list!

How much do you think these appliances cost to run?

To find out, you will need to know points 1) and 2) below.

1) How much electricity the appliance uses. This is measured in watts. You will find this information on the rating plate on the bottom or at the back of the appliance (figure 15).

You will see information about the volts (V), hertz (Hz), and watts (W).

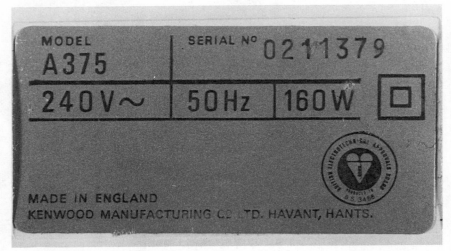

Figure 15   Electricity rating plate.

What do you notice about the Hz and V figures on your appliances? They give information about the mains electricity coming into the home. The pressure behind the flow of electricity is called the voltage. In Britain mains electricity is 240 V. Hertz is the unit used to show the frequency of the electricity – the number of complete cycles the voltage goes through each second. The Hz is an international unit for measuring and in Britain is about 50.

What do you notice about the wattage figure? Sometimes the figure is given in kilowatts (kw). To change all your kilowatts to watts multiply by 1000, *e.g.* 3.1 kw = 3100 watts.

2 The cost of electricity for your area. Do you know the name and address of your local electricity board? There are twelve of them, and they are responsible for providing your area with electricity which it buys in bulk from the Central Electricity Generating Board. You should be able to find the name and address in the local telephone directory or on an electricity bill. The cost per unit of electricity will be on your electricity bill too. A unit is one kilowatt (1000 watts) used for 1 hour, called a kilowatt-hour.

Make a table like this:

Appliance	Watts	Hours for which the appliance is used, *e.g.* 30 minutes/ 0.5 hours	Unit cost	Cost per hour

To calculate the running cost you will need to do the following sum:

$$\text{running cost} = \frac{\text{watts} \times \text{hours}}{1000} \times \text{cost of unit}$$

For example, a 500 watt iron used for 1 hour will cost 2 p if electricity is 4 p per unit.

$$\text{running cost} = \frac{500 \times 1}{1000} \times 4 = 2$$

You could use a calculator or a computer to help you to work out the cost of running all your electric appliances. Arrange them in order to show the most expensive to run.

If you are working out the running cost of something like a washing machine or freezer, which has a heater or motor that is not on all the time the appliance is in use, this sum will not be very accurate. Why not? How could you make your results more accurate?

Paying the electricity bill

The electricity used by a home is measured by a meter. This may look like the one in figure 16.

Or it may be a more modern meter showing just the figures, like the one shown in figure 17.

The meter is sometimes found indoors, usually near the front door. It belongs to the Electricity Board, who charge you to hire it, and you must let them in to read the meter. More and more homes now are being built with meters which can be read from the outside, and in time it is likely that our meters will be read by computer from the Board's headquarters.

To read the meter you read off the numbers on the dials. You will notice that the dials are numbered alternately clockwise and anticlockwise. If the hand lies between two numbers, read off the smaller number.

Figure 16   Electricity meter: dial type.   *Figure 17   Electricity meter: modern figure type.*

The reading on the meter in figure 18a is 15239. (Ignore the $\frac{1}{10}$ when reading the meter.)

Work out the readings shown on the meters in figure 18b. (Note that the $\frac{1}{10}$ dial has not been shown.)

Activity

Try reading your meter at home every day for a week. Take each day's reading away from the day before to find out how many units you have used. For example:

Reading on Wednesday night 11.30 p.m.	1412
Reading on Tuesday night 11.30 p.m.	1325
Units used on Wednesday	87

Did you use about the same number of units every day? If not, why do you think this might be? (Think about who is in the house, and at what times each day.)

Every quarter (three months) you may be sent a bill based on the readings. If you were out when the meter reader called, the Board may have to guess the figures, by looking at the number of units used on other bills. This is shown by an E for "estimated" on the bill. Once a year the Board will insist on reading the meter, though, and will make an appointment if necessary.

There are other ways to pay the bill, and these are shown on the other side of the electricity bill. What would be the advantages and disadvantages of the methods shown? (See the booklet *Understanding your electricity bill*.)

Figure 18

On the bill in the booklet you will see that a "standing charge" is made, and then a charge for the units used. It is possible to get electricity more economically than this by using the "off peak" rate. This is called Economy 7. Electricity used during the night can be about half the price and is ideal for night storage heaters, off-peak water heaters, or for leaving the washing machine or tumble dryer on at night. You will find that the standing charge is slightly higher and the day-time rate for electricity may be higher too with Economy 7.

Find out what the off-peak rate is for your area and what hours it is available.

The bill provides other useful information, for example how you can get help or advice with problems or complaints. The Electricity Council has a consultative council to look after the users. This is important with nationalised industries where you cannot walk in and talk to the manager as you do in a shop. Nationalised industries are those that are owned by the state. Generally they have no competition from other suppliers. This means that you don't have any choice. As far as fuel is concerned you do have the choice of using gas or coal, for example, instead of electricity, but there is only one supplier to get electricity or gas from.

Being cut off

If you do not pay your electricity bills you can be cut off and you will have to pay to be connected again. A code of practice drawn up by the Electricity Council and British Gas says that you will not be cut off if:

you are on Supplementary Benefit
you are getting Family Income Supplement
the breadwinner is unemployed
there are children under five in the family.

You must get in touch with the Gas or Electricity Board and the Social Security Officer or the Social Services Department immediately if you cannot pay.

Using electricity

The electricity coming into the home goes through a sealed fuse box. This is the property of the Electricity Board and must never be opened. The mains circuit then goes through the meter and into a mains fuse box where the mains circuit is split into smaller units so that the whole house can be supplied with heat and light. There is a mains switch by the side of this fuse box.

The mains circuit splits into smaller circuits each with its own fuse. One supplies the cooker, another the water heater, one the lighting, and one will probably be the ring mains. The ring mains goes from room to room and all the electric sockets are taken from it before it returns to the starting point. It makes fitting extra sockets easy. Most houses, except very small ones, have two ring mains, for example one upstairs and one down. There is a diagram of a ring mains circuit in figure 19.

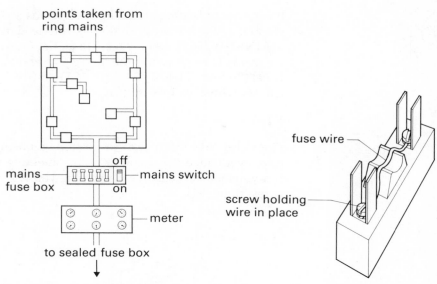

Figure 19   Ring mains circuit.

Figure 20   Mains fuse.

If a piece of electrical equipment is not working properly, or if you have too many appliances in one socket, one of the mains fuses could blow. The wire in it melts, which stops the flow of electricity. Try to find out what has caused the fuse wire to melt before mending it – think about which appliances were on at the time – had you just plugged something in? Turn these off.

To mend a mains fuse

1) TURN THE MAINS SWITCH OFF.

It is useful to keep a torch near the mains fuse box in case all the lights go off.
2) You may have a cartridge fuse which can be taken out and replaced, or the type which needs rewiring.

To rewire a fuse

Take out each fuse in turn. Look at the wire which stretches across inside it. If it has melted then it will need replacing.

The wire is held in place by two screws (figure 20).

Unscrew these and replace the wire with another piece of the same thickness. On the front of the fuse box it will say which wire to use. Fuse wire usually comes on a card in various thicknesses (figure 21).

Screw up tightly. Replace the fuse. Turn the electricity back on.

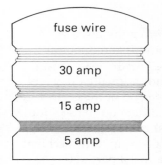

Figure 21   Fuse wire.

Activity

Practise wiring a fuse so that you can do it easily.

It is useful to label the fuses in the fuse box so that you know what will go off if a fuse is blown. To do this you need to **TURN OFF THE MAINS SWITCH**. Remove one fuse, then turn the mains switch back on again. Then go round the house and find out what is not working. Label the fuse. **TURN OFF THE MAINS SWITCH**. Replace the fuse. Do this with each fuse in turn.

Plugs

Plugs also have safety features to stop you being electrocuted if you have overloaded the circuit or used something with too high a voltage.

If you look at the inside of the plug you will find there are three wires (figure 22).

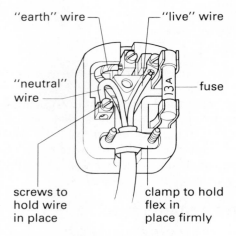

Figure 22   Inside a plug.

Two of these carry the electric current to and from the piece of equipment. They are called the "live" (brown or red) and "neutral" (blue or black) leads. The third wire is called the "earth" lead. It is coloured green and yellow or green, and does not normally carry any electric current. It is there as a safety device. One end of the earth wire is fastened to a metal part of the appliance, the other end to the middle pin of the three-pin plug. When the plug is pushed into the wall the middle pin is joined up to the earth of the house wiring. If by accident a live or neutral wire comes apart and touches a metal part of the appliance this part will become live. The electricity will go to earth through the quickest route – if you touched the appliance this would be you, and you would be electrocuted. The "earth" lead is an easier path for the electricity to go to earth. Because a large amount of electricity is going that way it blows the fuse, shutting off the electricity and making everything safe.

Activity

Practise wiring up a plug yourself. Figure 23 shows you how.
Check with your teacher that it is correctly wired up.

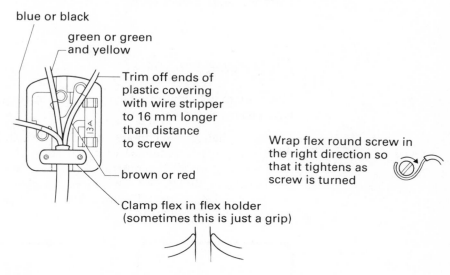

blue or black

green or green
and yellow

Trim off ends of
plastic covering
with wire stripper
to 16 mm longer
than distance
to screw

Wrap flex round screw in
the right direction so
that it tightens as
screw is turned

brown or red

Clamp flex in flex holder
(sometimes this is just a grip)

Figure 23   Wiring a plug.

Hair dryers do not have an earth because the parts carrying electricity inside are insulated with plastic coverings which do not let electricity pass through. The outside is plastic too, so it could not become live. Which other appliances would be like this?

It is important to fit the right size fuse, according to the wattage of the appliance. If the fuse's amperes are too high the appliance could be ruined before the fuse burnt out and could be dangerous. If the fuse's amperes are too low they could blow too often and this would be annoying, but not dangerous.

Choosing the right fuse

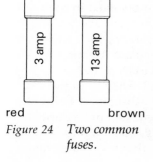

3 amp

13 amp

red   brown

Figure 24   Two common fuses.

The two most common fuses are shown in figure 24.

A 3-amp fuse (red) is used for appliances up to 720 watts, *e.g.* table lamp, hair dryer, electric blanket, food mixer, black and white television.

A 13-amp fuse (brown) is used for appliances from 720 to 3,000 watts, *e.g.* freezer, washing machine, electric fire, iron. Colour televisions and some appliances which have a motor (like a vacuum cleaner) need a 13-amp fuse even if they are below 720 watts. This is because there is a surge of electricity when they are first turned on.

Activity

In the table you made earlier you wrote down the wattage for each piece of equipment. You should now be able to write down the correct fuse to use in each.

Electricity and safety

There are many ways in which you can protect yourself from accidents when using electricity.

1) Buy appliances which have the BEAB (British Electrotechnical Approvals Board) trademark or its variation.
   A sample of products containing the mark in figure 25a will have been tested by BEAB, and the sample complies with legal requirements in the United Kingdom. (Electrical Equipment (Safety) Regulations, 1975, and its amendments.)

BEAB Approved

(a)

BEAB Approved via CCA

(b)

Figure 25
(a) Unregistered BEAB trademark.
(b) Variation of the unregistered BEAB trademark.

A sample of products containing the mark in figure 25b will have been tested and approved by another CCA approvals authority. They will have provided BEAB with test results and written information. BEAB will grant a licence, but will not have been involved in the testing or assessment.
   The CCA is the CENELEC Certification Agreement which was signed in 1983 by BEAB. Other countries involved are Austria, Belgium, Denmark, Finland, France, Germany, Ireland, Italy, Netherlands, Norway, Sweden, and Switzerland. They form the European Committee for Electrotechnical Standardisation (CENELEC).
   Power operated tools, like an electric drill, are tested by the British Standards Institution. They test goods for safety, quality, and reliability. They make spot checks to make sure that goods are still up

to scratch. Goods which pass the testing are given the Kitemark label (figure 26). Power tools will be marked with the Kitemark BS 2769 label.

2) Never let water and electricity come into contact. Do not touch electrical appliances with wet hands. (See figure 27.)

Figure 26   The Kitemark.

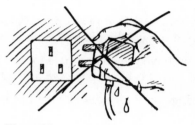

Figure 27

3) Do not overload adaptors. It is safer to put more sockets in the home. (See figure 28.)

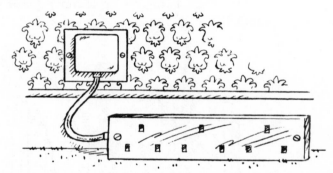

Use an extension board instead of overloading one socket

Figure 28

4) Do not trail flexes. You may trip over them, and they may become worn and dangerous. (See figure 29.)

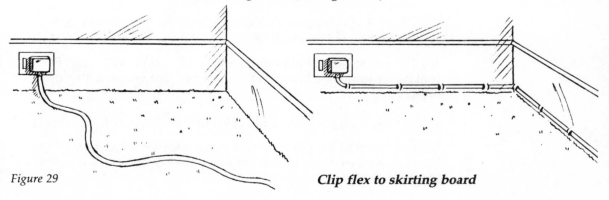

Figure 29   **Clip flex to skirting board**

Figure 30

5) Replace frayed flexes. (See figure 30.)

6) In bathrooms there should be pull switches for the light. There should not be sockets, except for shaver points. Electrical appliances should not be used in the bathroom. Heaters should be fixed, radiant wall heaters with a pull cord so that wet hands do not touch the switch.

7) If there are young children in the house fit sockets with plastic covers so that nothing can be pushed in.

8) Make sure you have the correct fuse for the appliance and that plugs are wired correctly. (See pages 48 and 49.)

9) Use light fittings only for lights. Do not plug in any other appliances.

10) Have the wiring circuit tested every five years. If wiring is more than 25 years old or the plugs have round pins the home will need rewiring.

11) Don't put clothes on top of convector or storage heaters. (See figure 31.)

Figure 31

12) Check that the wattage of bulbs in table lamps is correct for the type of shade used, to avoid fires.

13) If bread sticks inside a toaster switch off and unplug, and allow to cool before removing bread. Do not poke around inside with a metal object.

Activities

Bearing in mind the points above make a leaflet or posters
 i) for new parents to help them make the house safer for young children

ii) for residents of elderly people's flats

iii) for pupils starting to work in the Home Economics room.

Take each point in turn and see if it applies to the problem you are thinking about. For example, suppose you were considering safety in the garden. Number 1 would apply and you might wish to include something about choosing electric lawn mowers with a BEAB label. For number 2 think about where in the garden water might be found and how you could keep the electrical appliances away from it, *e.g.* do not cut the hedge after it has been raining. For number 4 think about how you could avoid trailing flexes in the garden or make it possible to work safely.

For each point try to find an example to illustrate your ideas.

Watch out in the newspapers for reports of accidents involving electricity. Try to work out what has gone wrong in each case.

SEE ALSO

Fuel
Gas } for information about other fuels for the home.
Energy saving for ways of saving energy.
Heating for methods of heating the home.
Lighting for use of electricity for lighting.

Further work on exploring electricity can be found in the "People and Homes" section of Nuffield Home Economics *Basic course* and *Teacher's guide*, Hutchinson, 1982.
Useful information may be obtained from the Electricity Council (address on page 180).

Energy saving

Send for energy saving leaflets from the Energy Efficiency Office, British Gas, and the Electricity Council. (Addresses on page 180.)

When you are feeling cold what do you do?

Put on another sweater? Turn the heating up, or stoke up the fire? Which of these will cost the most money?

Using fuel like gas, coal, oil, or electricity is expensive. Most people spend about 10 per cent of their income on fuel and a large amount of this money is wasted because our homes are losing heat.

Our sources of fuel are also running out, so we need to think carefully about the type of fuel we have and how we use it.

We use energy in the home for heat, light, and power for equipment. Saving some of this energy should save us money, and help to save the World's fuel resources.

Some ways of saving energy in the home are simple and we could all make a start on them today.

Discussion

How is energy being saved in each of the pictures in figure 32?

How is energy being wasted in the pictures in figure 33?

Which of the savings in figure 32 would cost no extra outlay of money?

Sometimes saving energy means spending money first, and you have to decide whether it is worth spending money now to save more (you hope!) in the future.

Activities

Find out how much it would cost to try the other ways of saving energy, *e.g.* measure round the door and window in your own bedroom and find out how much it would cost to put a draught-proof strip round.

Figure 32

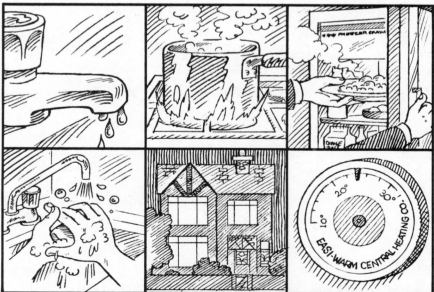

Figure 33

An energy audit

To find out if you use energy wisely you could carry out an energy audit. This means making a careful survey of your home, fuel bills, and equipment used in the home for heating, water heating, cooking, etc. You could then decide whether there are any ways in which you could save energy, and therefore money.

To help you collect and use this information you might want to use the computer program CEDRIC2 (see page 60). With CEDRIC2 you can compare the information you have gathered with the national average.

Here are some of the things you might consider:

1) The fuel bill
Read the gas and electricity meters every day for two or three weeks. Also write down how many buckets of coal and how much oil or paraffin you have used.

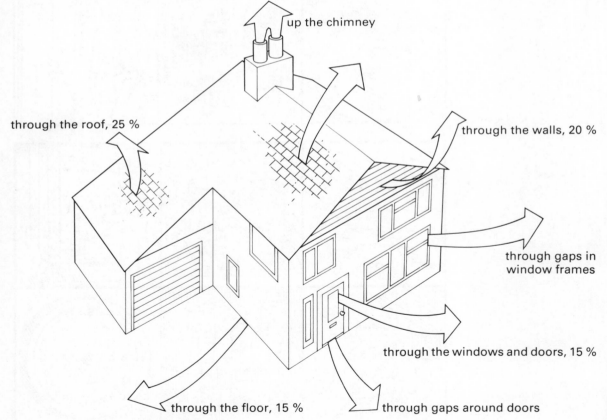

up the chimney

through the roof, 25 %

through the walls, 20 %

through gaps in window frames

through the windows and doors, 15 %

through the floor, 15 %

through gaps around doors

Figure 34   How a home loses heat.

2) The type of home

Draw some of the different types of home you could live in, for example maisonette, flat, detached, semi-detached, terraced, bungalow, cottage, caravan.

Heating a home can be expensive. About 70–80 p in the pound of a fuel bill can go on heating a home and providing hot water. This is because a lot of the heat is wasted. Figure 34 shows how a house loses heat.

Which of the types of home you have drawn do you think will lose the most heat? Why? Put them in order with the home likely to lose the most heat at the top.

3) Insulation

Insulation is the way in which you stop the heat escaping from a house as shown in figure 34.

Check whether you already have:

Loft insulation This is material which you put between the joists in the roof. It may be in loose beads (useful if the loft has corners which are difficult to get into as you can pour them in), or in a blanket form (figure 35). You will need to wear protective clothing and a face mask to prevent fibreglass insulation from being breathed in or getting into the skin.

Figure 35   Different types of loft insulation.

Roof insulation should be 100 mm (4 inches) thick to do much good. Measure yours.

Insulation on the hot water cylinder. You can buy a jacket to go over the hot water tank (figure 36). The tank should be measured carefully before buying one as these jackets come in different sizes.

Look for the Kitemark (figure 26, on page 51), which will guarantee that the jacket is made to a British Standard.

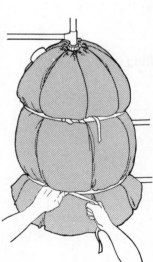

Figure 36 Insulation round the hot water cylinder.

Insulation round the pipes Water pipes in the loft may be insulated either by a wrapping of mineral or glassfibre matting, or you may have tube-like insulation which clips round the pipes (figure 37).

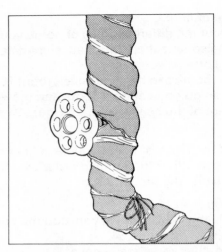
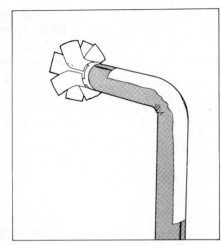

Figure 37   *Two types of insulation for the water pipes.*

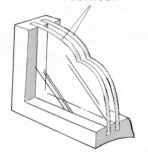

2 sheets of glass sealed with a space between

Figure 38   *Double glazing.*

4) Double glazing

Fifteen per cent of heat escapes through doors and windows. Double glazing can cut this loss down. Do you have double glazing (figure 38)? Is it the sort that has a plastic insert between the glass and the frame? (This provides extra insulation and is called a thermal break.) Or is it do-it-yourself secondary glazing?

Safety point: When installing double glazing think about how you would get out if there was a fire. Never have a room in which it is impossible to open all the windows. Remember that it is very difficult to break double-glazed windows.

5) Cavity wall insulation

Heat loss through walls can be cut down by filling cavity walls with

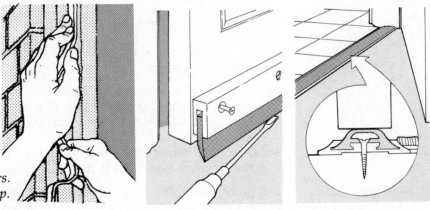

Figure 39 *Draught excluders.*
    (a) Adhesive strip.
    (b) and
    (c) Door seals. (a)   (b)   (c)

insulating foam or mineral fibre. Holes are drilled in the outer wall, and the foam or fibre is pumped through the holes into the "cavity" between the two walls. The holes are then sealed. You need to employ a firm which specialises in this work; you cannot "do-it-yourself".

6) Draught excluders
Draughts round door and window frames are usually cheap and easy to stop using a simple adhesive strip or screw-on seal (figure 39).

7) Equipment used
Make a list of all the equipment used in the home for cooking, water heating, heating, etc. Write down how long each is used for each day and at what setting.

Find out the cost of the different forms of insulation mentioned in parts 3, 4, 5, and 6. Arrange them in order of cost.

If the computer program CEDRIC2 is available compare the information you collected (in parts 1 to 7) with that of the national average.

Discussion

Are there any cheaper ways of making any of these energy-saving measures? For example if you cannot afford double glazing you could try draught-proofing the windows and using thicker curtains. Would your suggestions be as effective?

How could you save money when using equipment, for example by turning the thermostat down?

People on low incomes often cannot afford to spend very much money on energy saving measures.

Think about how the elderly could economise on fuel without endangering their health. Produce a leaflet to help them which could be distributed at old people's clubs.

SEE ALSO

Fuel for information about coal and oil.
Electricity for information about the cost of using equipment.
Gas for information about using gas as a fuel.

Useful information concerning energy saving may be obtained from the Electricity Council, British Gas, and the Energy Efficiency Office (addresses on page 180).
"CEDRIC2" computer program for the BBC or RML computer, available from British Gas Education Service (address on page 180).

Environment

Figure 40

Just one example of how the environment (surroundings) can be spoiled by thoughtless people is shown in figure 40.

Activity

Take a camera round your neighbourhood and photograph any other examples you can find, for instance graffiti on walls, smoke from a factory.

All these show the pollution of the environment. Pollution may be caused by smoke, litter, chemicals, oil, radioactivity, or noise.

Noise

Discussion

Think of the sort of situations in which noise might be a problem, such as ice cream van chimes, transistor radios. Can you think of any solutions to these problems?

Litter

Many pollution problems are caused by the large amount of rubbish we have to get rid of, in particular the amount of packaging in the form of paper bags, wrappers, plastic bags, cartons, cardboard boxes, etc.

Activity

Keep a record of what goes into your dustbin over the period of a week to find out how much waste is packaging, food waste, bottles, tins, etc. Make a poster to show how much waste you recorded.

Smoke

The Clean Air Act of 1956 ordered that, in some areas, no homes or factories can burn coal or any fuel which produces smoke. This was to stop smog forming. Smog was caused when smoke from chimneys could not escape into the air through thick fog. Smog made some people die from bronchitis and other diseases of the lungs. It is an offence to light a bonfire in a clean air zone.

Discussion

Is yours a clean air zone? If so why do you think this is?

Chemicals

Rivers may be polluted by factories discharging waste. This can often be seen in the form of scum, from detergent factories.

Oil

Disasters involving oil tankers cost thousands of pounds worth of damage and cause the death of wild life.

Activity

Find out what happened in the *Torrey Canyon* disaster in 1967 and the *Amoco Cadiz* in 1978. How could these disasters have been avoided?

Radioactivity

Under an Act of Parliament of 1960 permission must be obtained from the government if radioactive waste from nuclear power stations is to be got rid of.

Activity

Imagine that radioactive waste is to be dumped near to where you live. Write a letter to the newspaper against this proposal.

The European Community Environment Programme (ECEP)

The EEC (European Economic Community) has a programme for improving the environment. It is concerned with improving things which might be a risk to health, such as drinking water or contamination of food by mercury.

> **SEE ALSO**
>
> *Waste disposal* for more on disposing of rubbish, and how some waste may be recycled.
>
> Invite someone from the District Council to come and talk to you about waste disposal, tipping, the provision of skips for rubbish, and litter control.

Equipment

Send for the Electricity Council's electrical equipment data files to use with the "QUEST" computer package to find out about cookers, microwave cookers, refrigerators, freezers, dishwashers, washing machines, and dryers. This will help you to decide on priorities when buying, and points out safety and economy features. (Available from AUCBE, address on page 180).

Electrical equipment

Activity

Make a list of the large equipment you have at home, such as a cooker, washing machine, refrigerator. Which of these do you use every day, once a week or less often?

Here is a list of large electrical equipment for the home:

cooker
chest freezer
upright freezer
refrigerator
automatic washing machine
twin-tub washing machine
tumble dryer
spin dryer
dish washer
vacuum cleaner
microwave cooker.

Activity

Make your own list, like the one above, for the smaller electrical equipment for the home, for example a kettle. If you were setting up home for the first time which of these items would be absolutely essential? Find out how much it would cost to buy these.

Non-electrical equipment

Much of the equipment in the home is non-electrical, such as saucepans, knives, baking tins. We are going to look at just one of these in more detail. Saucepans need to cook well, clean easily, and stand up to hard usage in the kitchen.

They may be made of:

aluminium
stainless steel
vitreous enamel
Pyrosil
glass
copper
cast iron.

Activities

Find an example of each of the above list in the Home Economics room, at home, or in a shop, and describe what it looks like.

Which of the following ways would you clean each?

Brillo pads
Ajax
hot soapy water and dishcloth
pan brush
Scotchbrite

Devise a test to show which of the pans in figures 41 and 42 will be quickest to heat up on a gas and on an electric cooker.

Why do you think this is?

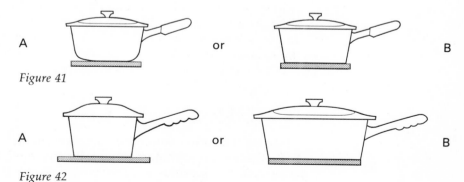

A   or   B

Figure 41

A   or   B

Figure 42

Which of the pans and lids in figure 43 will be easiest to clean and why?

Figure 43

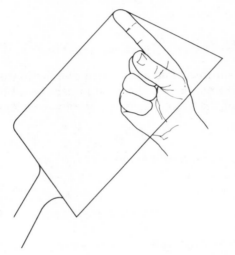

Figure 44

Try the finger-tip test to check whether food will be trapped in the inside curve of a saucepan.

The end of your first finger should fit right inside the curve between the bottom and side of the pan, as shown in figure 44.

Non-stick cookware

Non-stick cookware has a coating of polytetrafluoroethylene, PTFE for short. This is similar to the material in the nose cones of aeroplanes, and was developed as a result of space research. It is often known by trade names like Teflon. Do you know any others?

What special care will you need to take when cooking with and cleaning non-stick cookware?

Activity

Make a list of other small cooking equipment.

By the side of each item write E for essential, U for useful but not essential, or L for luxury.

SEE ALSO

Labelling
Shopping } for information about buying equipment.

Cookers
Freezers } for more about choosing large electrical equipment.
Refrigerators

See the book *Food for Health* (in this series) for more information about pressure cookers and slow cookers.

"QUEST" and the electrical equipment data files for the BBC or RML computer, available from AUCBE (address on page 180).

First aid

List the times that you can remember that you, or someone you know, has had an accident or injury.
What happened? What was done? Who helped?

A knowledge of simple first aid may be useful at times like these. The best way to feel ready to deal with any emergency is to enrol for a course in first aid with the Red Cross or St John's Ambulance.
This is a guide to simple treatment.

Cuts
Clean the wound with cool, running water, dry the skin with cotton wool, and cover with a clean dressing.

Small burns and scalds
Put under cold water to ease the pain. Pat dry and cover with a clean, dry dressing. Do not use fat, ointments, or creams. If burns or scalds are more serious seek medical help.

Fainting
If someone feels faint get them near fresh air and put their head between their knees. A drink of water may help. If someone actually faints offer reassurance, keep them lying flat, loosen tight clothing, and raise the legs slightly.

Nose bleeds
Tilt the head forwards to stop blood being swallowed. Gently squeeze the nostrils and allow breathing through the mouth.

Insect bites and stings
If the sting is still there remove it with tweezers. Smooth on anti-histamine cream or use bicarbonate of soda (or even spit) for bee stings, or vinegar for wasp stings.

Poisoning
Get medical help quickly. Keep the poison, if possible, and any vomit to show the doctor. The treatment will vary depending on what has

been swallowed. If there are red rings round the mouth give large amounts of milk or water.

Choking

Stand behind the person choking, put your arms around their waist and squeeze as hard as you can, pushing your hands into their stomach just below the ribs; **or** thump them on the back between the shoulder blades.

Shock

Any accident may be followed by shock, even some time after it has happened.

Do not give anything to drink; keep the patient warm, calm, and lying down. Give plenty of air and reassurance.

In an emergency you can call for help by dialling 999 for Fire, Police, or Ambulance.

It is possible to dial 999 easily in the dark. Feel for the last hole on the receiver with the middle finger of your right hand. Put your first (index) finger in the next hole. Keep it there and dial 9 three times. If you know someone who lives alone, such as an elderly relative or friend, it may be useful to show them how to do this.

Activities

Here is a list of items for first aid. Which would you keep
1) in the home   2) in the car   3) for use in accidents?

scissors	sterile bandages
plasters	lint
sterile dressings	notebook and pencil
cotton wool	antiseptic
safety pins	indigestion tablets
anti-histamine cream	crêpe bandage
throat lozenges	antiseptic wipes
tweezers	finger stall
thermometer	money or Phonecard

It is possible to buy first aid kits made up. Find out how much this would be and how much to make a similar kit up for yourself, buying the items individually.

Freezers

Figure 45   Different types of freezers.
(a) Chest
(b) Fridge-freezer.
(You can also have a
freezer-fridge.)
(c) Upright.

Collect manufacturer's leaflets for freezers.

Activities

Look at figure 92 on page 131.
  Answer these questions:
1) At what temperature does water freeze?
2) At what temperature does a refrigerator work?
3) At what temperature does a freezer work?
4) What is the difference between refrigerating and freezing food?
5) Why do you think it is possible to freeze commercially things like strawberries, which you cannot freeze successfully at home?

What are the different types of freezer in figure 45 called? Can you think of two advantages and two disadvantages of each?

A freezer may be placed anywhere convenient which is cool and dry and where a 13-amp power point is available. It is sometimes difficult to find room for a chest freezer in the kitchen. Can you think of two other places it might be kept?

How a freezer works

The freezer cabinet is kept cool by a liquid refrigerant absorbing heat from the cabinet and foods. The liquid changes into a vapour when warm. This vapour is forced into a condenser by power from the compressor (a kind of pump powered by an electric motor). Here it gives off heat (into the room) and becomes a liquid again to pass back into the evaporator.

The symbol in figure 77, on page 112, indicates that the freezer, or freezing compartment of a refrigerator, is suitable for freezing a stated weight of fresh food daily, following the manufacturer's instructions, and is also suitable for the storage of freshly frozen and commercially prepared foods.

Freezing foods

When food is frozen the aims are:
1) To get out as much air as possible from packages.
   This is done by squeezing bags tightly.
2) To stop the action of enzymes which might spoil flavour or texture.
   This is done by blanching. This means putting fruit or vegetables into boiling water for a few minutes, then into cold water to prevent the food cooking.
3) To prevent large ice crystals from forming.
   Large ice crystals can give food an unpleasant texture. Dry food in a cloth or paper towel before freezing to prevent ice crystals.
4) To wrap or cover food to stop drying out.
   Correct packaging is important to prevent food from drying out and to stop flavours transferring from one food to another.
5) To lower the temperature so that microorganisms causing decay stop working.
   The fast-freeze switch must be put on when putting food in the freezer.

Packaging

Activities

To find out which is the best packaging material for foods in the freezer try out the following test.

You will need
   food to be tested, *e.g.* meat, fruit, vegetables, liquids (e.g. stock)
   a selection of packaging materials, *e.g.* foil, clingfilm, plastic containers, greaseproof paper (you could find out what is available from your local freezer centre and shops).

1) Prepare the food for the freezer in the usual way.
2) Wrap or package the food in a variety of different ways. Make sure as much air is removed as possible and seal.
3) Put one sample of each food, uncovered, on a dish or foil tray.
4) Put items in the fast-freeze compartment and put the switch on fast freeze for the recommended time.
5) Examine after 1 week, 1 month, 3 months.
   What does this tell you about the different materials used for packaging?

What would you freeze in the following:

rigid plastic containers
polythene bags
waxed cartons
clingfilm
foil wrap
foil containers?

All packages must be well sealed. For this you can use special adhesive tape, lids, or wire closures.

Labelling

Food in the freezer can look the same, so clear labelling is essential.

Activity

List four pieces of information which would be useful on the label.

Using frozen foods

Most foods need thawing before use (except thin pieces of meat and fish and some baked items).

Once thawed microorganisms become active again, so foods should be treated as if they were fresh foods.

DO NOT REFREEZE THAWED FOODS. (Foods frozen raw and then cooked may be frozen again after cooking.)

SEE ALSO

Refrigerators for information about keeping foods cold.

Fuel

We need fuel in the home to provide the energy for light, heating, and power. Fuels used most often in the home are gas, electricity, coal, and oil. Coal, oil, and natural gas are not replaced when they are burnt, so there is a chance that we will, at some time, run out. Other fuels are being tried to replace them.

What sources of fuel are shown in figures 46 and 47?

Figure 46 Modern windmill at the Centre for Alternative Technology, Machynlleth, Wales.

Figure 47 These solar panels on a terraced house can provide about half the hot water a family needs.

Conduct a survey within your class to find out which are the most popular forms of fuel.

You may be able to compare the cost of using different fuels for heating or cooking using one of the computer programs which has been written to help you to do this. (There is a list of these at the end of this section.)

There are separate topics in this book on gas and electricity, and also on heating, lighting, and saving energy, so here we are just going to look at the use of oil and coal.

Discussion

What are the advantages and disadvantages of using coal or oil as a fuel?

Things to think about:
Cost (Will it be possible to shop around for the lowest price? Is it possible to buy more cheaply in the summer?)
Where you live
Storage
Cleanliness
How to avoid running out of supplies
Who is in the home and when?
Pollution

Safety with coal

Fires can start easily if sparks jump out onto a rug or carpet, or if the fire is built up so high that the chimney can catch fire. So keep the size of the fire under control.

Care is needed too by the people near fires. What are the three major dangers shown in figure 48?

Did you know it is an offence to leave a child of under five alone in a room with an unguarded fire?

Safety with oil stoves

Oil stoves are often used because they are cheap to run.
They are safe to use when they are properly looked after, but they need careful attention.

Figure 48

*They should stand level on the floor where there is no danger of them being knocked over.
*There should not be a strong draught, but some air is needed for the stove to burn well.
*They should not be moved when alight.
*There should be a strong fireguard around the stove if there are children in the home.

SEE ALSO

Electricity
Gas } for information about other fuels.
Heating for information about heating a home.
Lighting for information about electric lighting.
Energy saving for information about using fuel.
Environment for more about fuel and the environment.

Computer programs which can be used to compare energy consumption:
"Watts in your home", available from Cambridge University Press (address on page 180).
"Home heating", available from Longman Micro Software (address on page 180).
"CEDRIC2", available from British Gas Education Service (address on page 180).

Furnishings

 Collect samples of flooring, of curtain materials, and from wallpaper books.

Furnishings, for example cushions, curtains, floor and wall coverings, provide comfort and a pleasant appearance, and also heat and noise insulation in a home.

It is often the choice of a pot plant or a brightly coloured cushion or rug which makes a house or rented room into a home.

Floor coverings

These are some of the floor coverings available:

carpets (wool, synthetic, *e.g.* acrylic, cord)
lino
carpet tiles
rugs
vinyl tiles
rush matting
cork tiles
cushion-floor

There are photographs of them in the colour section, between pages 106 and 107.

Activities

Find out what each of the floor coverings in the list above looks like, how they are bought (in a pack, by the metre), and how much they cost to buy.

How will they wear?

Here is a test you could try on different types of lino, vinyl, or cork tiles, and on cushion-floor. You will need small samples of each for testing.
1) Resistance to pressure (this will show how they might be marked, by, for example the heels of shoes, furniture being moved).

Try marking each floor covering with a skewer, as shown in figure 49. Which is the most resistant?

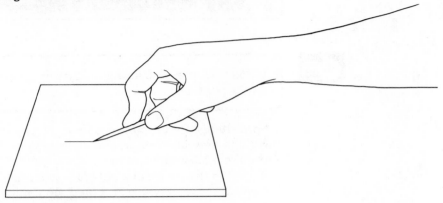

Figure 49

2) Resistance to scratching (for example children's toys being run backwards and forwards).

Rub a piece of each floor covering with wire wool for one minute. Which shows the least scratch marks?

How will you clean them?

Make a piece of each floor covering dirty, for example with mud or spilt food.

Clean a sample of each floor covering with:
 i) a sponge and Flash
 ii) a cloth and water
iii) scouring powder and a scrubbing brush.

Which cleans the best?

Clean a piece of each with:
 i) wax polish
ii) liquid polish.

What do you think it would be like walking in socks on these surfaces? What advice would you give about polished floors and safety?

In groups, make up some similar tests to the ones above for testing carpets for wear and cleaning. Present your results to the rest of the class and decide who carried out the best research.

Which floor covering would you use for:

the kitchen   the hall and stairs
the living room   the bathroom?
a child's bedroom

Window coverings

Some of the coverings you could use for windows are:

curtains
venetian blinds
roller blinds
vertical blinds.

Activities

What materials are suitable for curtains? Find out the cost of making curtains for your own room at home and compare it with the cost of venetian, roller, or vertical blinds.

Devise a test to show why curtains may be lined.

Which window coverings will be most suitable for:

the kitchen
the living room
the bathroom
the bedroom?

Bedding

Activity

Find out the size of a single bed and a double bed.
    You may choose to have:
sheets, pillow cases, blankets, eiderdown, bedcover
or a duvet with duvet cover, bottom sheet, and pillow cases.
    Find out how much it would cost to fit out a single bed with each of these alternatives.
    What do you think are the advantages/disadvantages of each?
    Find out what the "tog" rating on a duvet means.

Wallcoverings

You may choose from:

paint
wallpaper
lining paper, painted
hessian
anaglypta.

Activities

From the wallpaper books collect a sample of each of these and arrange in order of cost:

small pattern
large pattern
washable
flocked
embossed
plain
mix 'n match.

Choose a sample of wallpaper suitable for:

your bedroom
the kitchen
a child's bedroom
the living room.

What factors are important in choosing the right sort of paper for these?

SEE ALSO

Colour schemes for more about colour when choosing furnishings.

See the book *Textiles for People* (in this series) for more about different types of materials, and making curtains.

Furniture

Activity

Imagine you are about to set up home in a bed-sitter on your own. Make a list of the items of furniture which you think you would not be able to do without.

What additional things would you need if you were a family in a ground-floor flat with a young baby and a toddler?

Where could you buy these in your town or main shopping centre?

Your list might include a chain store such as the Co-op, a department store, discount warehouse, or small shop. You may have thought of a mail order catalogue too. Choose one of your items of furniture and make a list of advantages and disadvantages for buying from each shop.

Find out how much it would cost for your first list of furniture from two or three different shops.

How will you decide which to buy?

Suppose you are going to buy a kitchen chair. You might think about:

Size   Will it fit under the table? Will it take up too much space?
Colour   Does it match, or go well with the table? Does it go with the decorating in the room?
Wear   Has it got a finish which will mark easily? Will children's toys dent it? How will it look after a couple of years' family use?
Cleaning   How will you keep it clean? If the baby spills food on it will it wipe clean?
Quality   Is it well made? Look at the way it has been joined together. Is it just glued, or made with proper joints? When you sit on it does it feel firm, not rocky? Are there any labels which might show that it has been tested for quality or workmanship, for example the Design Centre or Kitemark labels?
Payment   How can you pay – cash, H.P., etc?
Delivery   Can it be delivered? How much will this cost? How long will you have to wait?

Activity

Choose another item of furniture from your list and make a check-list for buying like the one for the kitchen chair.

As furniture is such an expensive item it is worth looking for second-hand items in shops, at auctions, or through advertisements in the paper. With a new coat of paint or varnish or new fabric to replace the old, it is possible to make things almost as good as new again. Avoid second-hand bedding though, as it can carry diseases.

Activities

How do you think you could renovate the pieces of furniture in figure 50?

Figure 50

When you have worked through this topic and the topic on *Furnishings* you will be able to try these projects:
1) You are about to move into the unfurnished room which is shown in the scaled plan in figure 51.

Room plan

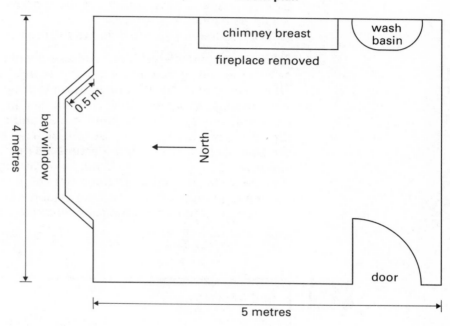

Bay window – front elevation

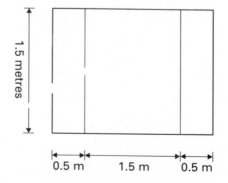

height of room: 3 metres

Figure 51

a) What furniture or fittings would be needed to make it into a bed-sitting room? Draw these on the plan. Indicate which would be new and which second-hand.

b) Explain and show on the diagram the colour scheme you would use, giving reasons for your choice.

c) List your considerations for choice of floor covering and indicate which you would choose.

d) If you were to have curtains at the window how much fabric would be needed?

e) List two items you could add to the room to make it welcoming.

2) The local council has hired you as a design consultant for some new homes being built in partnership with a housing company. They want you to furnish one of these to show in photographs and the newspapers but will only use your design if it is the cheapest to carry out. To start with you have to plan and cost the decoration and furnishing of a sitting room, likely to be used by a lone parent and pre-school child. The room measures 3.6 m × 3.9 m. It has a window 1.5 m × 1.2 m. There will be no dining room in the flat. Prepare a scaled diagram of the room and indicate the fabrics, furniture, and furnishings, and the colours you plan to use. Cost this out. Add drawings and samples to illustrate your work.

SEE ALSO

Labelling for more about how to assess the quality of a piece of furniture.

Paying for goods for more about HP.

Gas

Send for leaflets about particular appliances, e.g. home heating, water heating, and cooking, and about reading the meter and using gas safely, from British Gas (address on page 180).

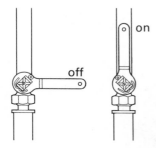

Figure 52 Mains gas tap.

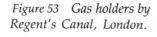

Figure 53 Gas holders by Regent's Canal, London.

Do you know

1) Which gas region you are in?
2) Where the mains gas tap is in your home?

You should be able to find out the answer to 1) from the telephone directory or from your gas bill.

Have a look for the mains gas tap if you do not know where it is. You may need to find it quickly in an emergency. It is usually near the gas meter. Make sure you know how to turn it off (figure 52).

When turning on the gas make sure that all appliance taps and pilot lights are turned off first. It is a good idea to keep a torch near the gas tap in case you have to find it in the dark.

Gas comes from the bed of the North Sea. It is piped underground and stored in gas holders like the ones in figure 53. Then it can be carried through underground pipes round a town.

Gas used to be made from coal, when it was known as coal gas or town gas.

North Sea gas is also sometimes called natural gas.

Activity

List all the gas appliances you might have in a home. Make a list of the advantages and disadvantages of having gas, for these, rather than electricity or any other fuel.

When buying gas appliances look for the BSI (British Standards Institution) label (figure 54).

Figure 54   BSI safety mark.   *Figure 55   British Gas label.*

This label shows that gas appliances and light fittings are safe to use.

British Gas also have a label which shows that appliances have passed their standards for reliability and fitness for purpose (figure 55).

What do you think is meant by "fitness for purpose"?

All gas appliances should be fitted by a qualified gas fitter. Gas Board employees are qualified, and so are members of CORGI (Confederation for the Registration of Gas Installers). There is a list of CORGI members in the British Gas showroom.

Laws about gas

Because gas can be dangerous there are laws about how to use it.

If you think gas is leaking you must turn off the supply. (This is why you need to know where your mains tap is.) Do not smoke or look for the gas tap or the leak with a lighted match or candle – why not? You must not use equipment that is unsafe or let anyone else use it.

You must tell your local gas service centre immediately if an escape of gas continues after you have turned off at the mains. There is an emergency number in case this is when the service centre is closed, and you should know the number to ring. Find out the number from the telephone book if you don't know it.

You must not turn on the gas, or any appliance, again until the escape or the appliance has been repaired.

You must not interfere with the pipes or meters which belong to British Gas.

If you break the laws concerned with the use of gas you could be fined up to £400.

If you smell gas in the street you should report it, too.

If you go into a house where there is a smell of gas open all the doors and windows, and then turn off the gas at the mains.

Gas appliances need air to work. When there is enough air the burning gas makes *carbon dioxide* which is harmless. If there is not enough air getting to appliances *carbon monoxide* will be formed. This is poisonous. Air is often provided by ventilators like those in figure 56.

Figure 56 Different types of ventilator.

(a) For windows.

(b) An air brick for wall ventilation.

Never block these up. You may have seen reports in the newspaper of people who have suffocated to death in their sleep, because they have blocked up all the air entry places in the house. Appliances should be serviced at least every two years, especially gas fires and central heating boilers, as soot can clog up the air passages too.

Paying for gas

The amount of gas used in a home is measured on the gas meter in cubic feet. This may be changed to cubic metres. The meter will either look like the one in figure 57, or it may be the newer style which can be read straight off (figure 58).

Figure 57   Gas meter: dial type.
If you ignore the top two dials, the
reading on this meter is 4105.

Figure 58   Gas meter: modern figure type.

You will probably find your gas meter near the front door, or it may be in a box on the wall so that it can be read from outside. If it is inside you must let the person from the Gas Board in to read the meter. (You should first ask the person for identification.)

Activity

Try reading your own meter. Ignore the top two dials and read off the numbers on the others. If the hand is between two numbers read the smaller number, unless it is between 0 and 9 in which case read 9. When you have the four-figure number add two noughts. This is now your meter reading in cubic feet.

Try reading the meters in figure 59.

The meter is read every quarter (three months). The price is worked out by the therm. To change the cubic feet into therms you need to know the calorific value and this is shown on the bottom of the bill. Use the number given in B.t.u. (British thermal units). A gas bill is shown in figure 60.

The sum you need to do is this:

$$\frac{\text{calorific value} \times \text{hundreds of cubic feet}}{1,000} = \text{therms}$$

Figure 59

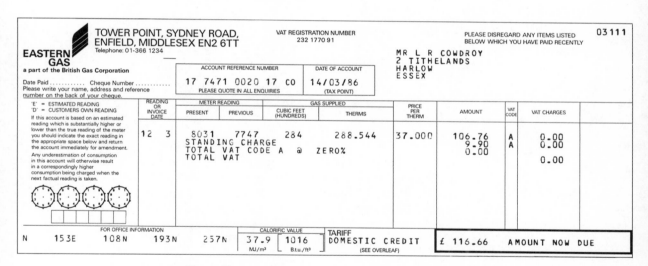

Figure 60

Check the figures on the gas bill with this calculation. Does it work out?

If you want to you can pay your gas bill through a budget scheme in equal monthly installments based on the amount of gas you usually use. The account is settled every year and under or over payment sorted out. You may also have a prepayment meter. You pay for gas in advance with this and the meter is emptied quarterly. It is also possible to buy savings stamps to use to pay the bill.

Discussion

What would you say were the advantages and disadvantages of each method of payment?

You must pay the gas bill within 28 days, or you may be given seven days' notice that you will be cut off. There are the same special exceptions as for electricity. You will have to pay for being cut off and reconnected.

SEE ALSO

Fuel for information about other fuels, *e.g.* coal, oil.
Electricity for general information, and for a list of people specially excepted from being cut off.
Energy saving for information about ways of saving fuel.

Visit your local British Gas showroom.

Heating

Activities

Several ways of heating a home are shown in figure 61, below and on the next page.

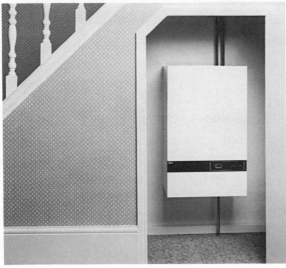

Figure 61   (part)

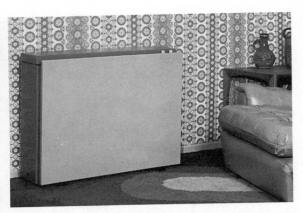

Figure 61   (continued)

Match them with the following:
1) Hard work.
2) Welcoming.
3) Easy to light.
4) Can be moved around.
5) Expensive to run for long periods or in large areas.
6) Heats water as well.
7) Not attractive to look at.
8) Allows heat to be wasted up chimney.
9) Can be timed to turn on and off when you are not there.
10) Storage space is needed for fuel.
11) Warms a room quickly.
12) Can make use of off-peak electricity.
13) Causes air pollution.
14) Cheap to run.

Figure 61   (continued)

These fuels may be used to heat a house:

gas   calor gas
electricity   paraffin
oil   coal.

Which fuel does each of the forms of heating in figure 61 use?

In the topic on *shopping* there are some ideas to think about when buying goods. Choose one of your forms of heating and make a check-list for buying.

SEE ALSO

Energy saving for saving energy when heating.
Electricity, Gas, and *Fuel* for more about the fuels used.
Labelling for more about safety labels to look for when buying.

Homes

Not everyone is fortunate enough to have a home of their own. Some people share accommodation and others do not have a roof over their heads at all.

Renting a home

Council house or flat

Council houses are houses provided by the local authority for a reasonable rent. If you rent a council house you are a council tenant. Some councils will pay for repairs to your house and may even modernise it, or add central heating; but it will never be your own unless the council decides to sell it to you.

You may have to wait a long time before getting a council house to rent. Some councils have a points scheme. This may give some people with special needs, for example a young family in crowded conditions, the chance to get a house more quickly.

Activity

If there is a Housing Advice Centre near you, you may be able to find out how the council house list works. Find out how long people have to wait for a house, and if there is a points system.

Discussion

Why do you think high-rise council flats like those in figure 62 were built? This type of housing has not been found to be very popular and is not built as much now. What might the disadvantages be? (Imagine you are a parent with a young baby, or a senior citizen.)

Renting privately from landlord

Houses, flats, and bed-sitting rooms can also be rented privately, either furnished or unfurnished from a landlord or landlady. Rents are usually higher than council rents. You may find advertisements for this type of home in a newspaper or in a newsagent's window (figure 63).

Figure 62   These blocks of high-rise flats are in Shepherd's Bush, in West London.

SHARE A FLAT

ROOM TO LET – close to city centre; £35 pw; 25+; m/f. 343 6089.

3-bed HOUSE to let; £120 pw; 3–4 persons; refs reqd. 569 7879.

LGE RM in friendly hse; £150 pcm incl. 456 5232.

Figure 63

Sometimes there can be arguments with a landlord/landlady about noise, notice to leave, or the rent you pay for furnished accommodation. If you cannot sort this out you may need the help of a rent tribunal. The address will be in the phone book. A rent tribunal will fix a fair price for a furnished flat or room and the owner cannot increase it. The Rent Officer sets a fair rent if the house or flat is unfurnished. His/her address will also be in the phone book. As a tenant you are protected by the Rent Act, which means that the owner cannot raise the rent unreasonably or cause discomfort or inconvenience.

Discussion

Often rented accommodation is shared.
    What are the advantages and disadvantages of sharing a home?

Lodgings

In lodgings a landlord/landlady will cook meals, clean the room, and change and wash the sheets. This saves you trouble, but it may mean you can be less independent. There may be set times for coming in at night or rules for entertaining visitors.

Hostels

Larger towns or cities may have hostels such as the Y.M.C.A. or Y.W.C.A. Details can be found at the Citizens Advice Bureau or a local library. There is often a big demand for hostels as they provide heat, hot water, meals, and company. They can be expensive.

You should be given a rent book for any rented accommodation (figure 64).

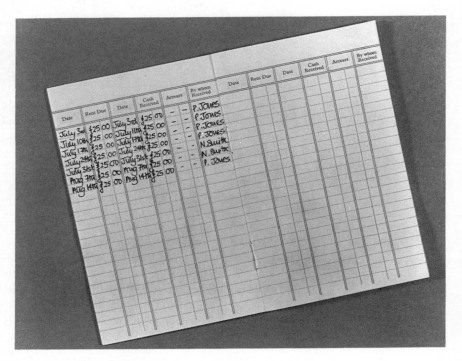

Figure 64   Rent book.

This is your proof that you have paid the rent so it should be kept somewhere safe.

Finding a home

Around the area where you live there will probably be a variety of different homes for rent or sale.

Activity

Illustrate or list the types of accommodation which are near to you.

When houses are advertised for sale or rent a special language is used to describe them. Words are shortened to save money in advertising, for example:

Semi-det. res. nr. schls. shops. 2 bed liv. rm. spac. kitchen

Det. hse. nr town ctre. 3 bed. 2 recep. gar. sep bath/wc. lge kit. ch. gdn

Thd. gl to shr. lge. flat. own rm. ckg. fac

Activity

List the shortened words (abbreviations) and what you think they mean. For example:

det. = detached (a house which is not joined to another one)

gdn = garden

Advertisements often leave out the things which are not very good, for example "near the motorway"; and they make other things sound better than they are, for example "very compact" could mean "small".

Activities

Write an advertisement for your own home or the home of someone you know in the way it would probably appear in an advertisement.
OR
Imagine you are an estate agent with a very dilapidated cottage in the country to sell. Write an advertisement to make it sound attractive. Don't tell any lies, but play down its undesirable features and emphasise the good points.

When you are choosing a home there are many things to think about. Arrange these in the order you think would be most important for you:

Near shops
Near place of work
With central heating
Old house needing a lot of work on it, but cheap
Near cinema, leisure centre, theatre or other entertainment
Near school
Near to countryside or park or other open space
With garage
Near transport – buses or trains
Modern house which won't need much decorating
Near doctor, dentist
With double glazing
Near church
With garden
Near library
Sunny rooms

   Which do you think would be most important for a family with two young children, or a senior citizen?

Make a list of the things you would avoid when buying a home.

When you have a rough idea of what you are looking for in a house you will probably go to an estate agent. Estate agents buy and sell property and will send you a list of properties which match what you are looking for. They do not charge for this, but will charge if you sell your house.

Activities

Look in the estate agent's windows and find out the cheapest and most expensive house on offer. Describe what you would be getting for your money.

Write a list of the advantages and disadvantages of the following:

Living on your own or in lodgings ("digs").
Sharing a rented, furnished flat with one or more friends.
Living at home with your family.

Elderly people often like to continue living in their own homes even when they find it difficult to cope.

What difficulties might be experienced by an elderly person living alone?

What alternative forms of accommodation are there?

What would be the advantages and disadvantages of having an elderly relative living with you?

Sharing a home with someone who is handicapped can put extra strains on a family. How could you help to make life easier for someone with a disability?

SEE ALSO

Mortgages for information about paying for a house.
Rates to find out about the services for which you pay the local authority.

Invite someone from Shelter or a similar organisation to talk to you about what it means to be homeless.

Insurance

 Collect application forms for different kinds of insurance.
Send for the Office of Fair Trading booklet *It might never happen but* . . . (address on page 180).

Figure 65

Figure 66

The people in figures 65 and 66 are taking a risk, something we all do from time to time. What risks do you take in your daily life? It is possible to pay a sum of money to protect yourself against events which may or may not happen. This is called insurance. You can insure against the chance of it raining on the day of a special event such as a village fête, or against the possibility of your home burning down. Some footballers even insure their legs against breaking.

You pay a sum of money (a premium) to an insurance company for an insurance policy. For insuring people against accidents or death insurance companies have a rating system to work out how hazardous different occupations are. A racing car driver would be more at risk than a shop assistant and would have to pay a higher premium.

██████ **Activity** ██████

Make a list of different occupations. Arrange them in order with the most dangerous at the top.

House insurance

This insures the fabric of a house.

This will protect you against loss caused by theft, fire, storm, flood, burst pipes, or other disasters. It also covers you for personal liability, for example if someone trips up on a loose stone on your path.

House contents insurance

New for old policy
This covers the full cost of replacing your possessions, however old they are. It is usually expensive.

Indemnity policy
This policy will cover the cost of replacing your possessions with others in the same condition.

All risks insurance
Most insurance policies do not cover you against everything that can happen. All risks policies insure things of special value, for example a fur coat, expensive video equipment. They can also give insurance cover for cash you are carrying on you when away from home.

Find out more about household insurance from the booklet *It might never happen but* . . .

Car insurance

By law anyone driving a car must be insured by a policy which at least covers the driver against claims for death or injury to others, including any passengers.

Third party cover
This also covers any damage you may do to other people's cars or property.

Comprehensive insurance
This policy covers damage to your own car. If an accident is someone else's fault you may be able to claim against their third party insurance.

No claims bonus
If you do not make a claim against your car insurance the premium will be reduced by a certain percentage the next year. After a certain number of years you get the maximum percentage discount.

Excess

If you are a young driver (under 25) you may have to pay the first £25 or £50 of a claim. This sum is called the excess. This is because there is a greater risk of a young and inexperienced driver having an accident.

Activities

Try to get hold of insurance forms and practise filling them in. Find out the meaning of any words you do not understand.

What are the most unusual forms of insurance that you can think of (for example insuring against the possibility of twins)?

Make a list of all the items you possess. How much would it cost to replace them?

Collect some leaflets from different insurance companies for the same thing, for example car insurance, house contents. Work out which would be the cheapest and which the most expensive.

Imagine that you and a group of friends are going to organise a disco. What would you need to insure against?

SEE ALSO

Assurance for providing for events which you know will happen one day.

Kitchen planning

Draw a plan of a kitchen – either your own or the kitchen of someone you know – on the planning grid supplied with the computer program TASK, or on a grid like the one in figure 67.

On the TASK grid sheet the side of one large square equals 25 cm. If you make your own grid you will need to work out the scale.

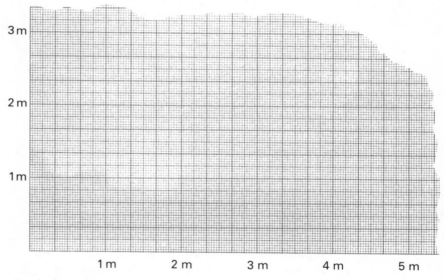

Scale: 1 cm = 0.5 m

Figure 67

Most work in the kitchen involves food and is carried out in this order:

storage → preparation → washing → cooking → serving

For this you need to move from:

storage area → work surface → sink → cooker → work surface

If these areas are placed close together you will not need to walk too far when carrying out tasks in the kitchen.

Activity

Put the five areas mentioned above into your kitchen trying to arrange them in a work triangle like the one in figure 68, or in a run like the one in figure 69.

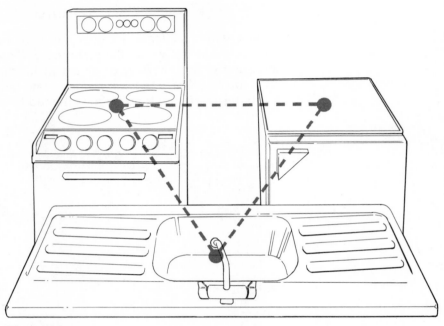

Figure 68

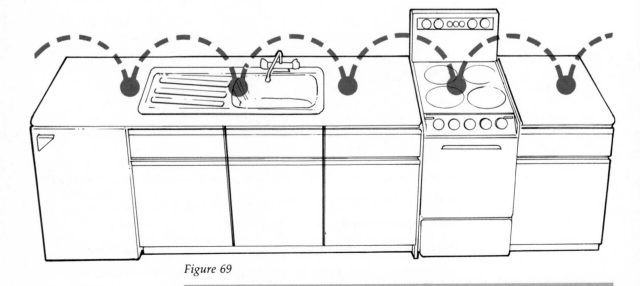

Figure 69

You may also need some of the following in your kitchen:

floor cupboards	spin dryer
wall cupboards	boiler
drawer units	dishwasher
refrigerator	table
freezer	chairs/stools
washing machine	cooker hood
tumble dryer	

Activities

If you were setting up home on a low budget which of these do you think would be absolutely necessary?
   Draw these on your kitchen plan.

Redraw the kitchen plan for a couple with two children who do a lot of entertaining and have a reasonable income;
OR
for a couple with two young children who have no separate dining room.

On one of the kitchens you have planned mark the safety points you have taken into consideration, for example, sockets and cooker switches out of reach of young children, doors opening so that you do not walk into them, cooker away from the window, power points away from taps.

You may be able to use a planning board or computer program to help you plan your kitchen. With the TASK computer program you will also be able to see the walls of the kitchen which will help with placing wall cupboards and looking at the position of gas, electricity, and water.
   With the TASK computer program you can also measure the distance walked, and the stretch into cupboards needed to carry out a task in the kitchen, by noting down your path from unit to unit, or appliance, in the kitchen. Using economy of movement in a kitchen is called ergonomics. Testing the ergonomics of your kitchen should show you if you spend a great deal of time walking from one side of the kitchen

to the other, or round items. It is also possible to do this by measuring with a length of thread on your plan, but it won't be as accurate and you won't be able to include the stretch.

SEE ALSO

Equipment for more on choosing large and small equipment for the kitchen.

TASK (Testing Assessment and Study of Kitchens), a kitchen planning program, available from British Gas Education Service (address on page 180).
Gas Planning Board, also available from British Gas.
The All Electric Kitchen, a booklet available from the Electricity Council (address on page 180).

H

I

M

Q

R

S

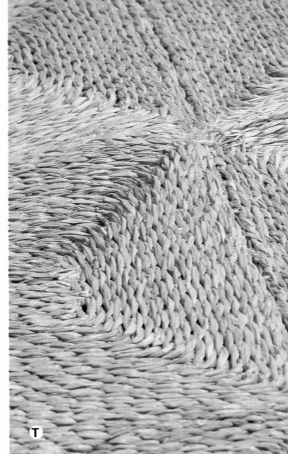

T

U

V

Labelling

Collect labels from food packets and tins, furniture, electrical goods, or other items around the home.
Send for the "Picture and Fact File", available from BSI Sales Department (address on page 180).

Labels are attached to things we buy to give information about:
1) Ingredients, weight, size, sell-by date, country of origin; *e.g.* food labelling.
2) How much energy an appliance is using, for example the input and output of a microwave cooker, the miles per gallon (or litre) on new cars. This is called energy labelling.
3) Washing or dry cleaning and fabric content, *i.e.* care labelling.
4) Testing for such things as safety and reliability, *i.e.* safety and quality labelling.

Activity

Sort the labels you have collected into these four groups.

You will probably have found some of these labels:

1) Food labels

Most foods must show:
*A list of ingredients in order (with the one there is most of at the top).
*A description of the product which people will understand.
*The name and address of the packer, labeller, or person in this country responsible for packing and labelling.
*The country of origin.

Activity

Take one of your food labels and indicate where each of these is to be found on the label. Is there any other useful information? It is expected that laws will soon be passed which will demand more information about the nutritional content of foods. List the information which you think would be useful on your label.

In the list of ingredients in food even added water must be shown, if there is more than 5 per cent. Food additives must also be shown.

Additives are things which are added to foods to alter the colour, taste, or texture, or to make foods last longer. After January 1986 all substances which are safe to add to food (except flavourings) had to have an E number, and this is shown on the list of ingredients. For example, if a label has E102 in the list of ingredients it will show that there is a yellow colouring called tartrazine.

Some people are allergic to food additives. Tartrazine can cause skin rashes or breathing problems. So labelling the additives will help people to avoid those which upset them.

Figure 70   Bar code from a tin of meat.

Bar codes, like the one in figure 70, can be seen on many items, for instance tinned foods. They will eventually appear on most items sold in supermarkets. A bar code can be read automatically when passed over a scanner. The information is sent to a central computer which sends back the price so that it can be printed with the food name on the till roll. The stock order can also be immediately updated. (*N.B.* A bar code does not show the price. It is in the computer that the prices are stored.)

2) Energy labels

A star symbol (figure 71) shows the octane rating of petrol and has to be shown on all pumps. Petrol may be 2, 3, or 4 star.

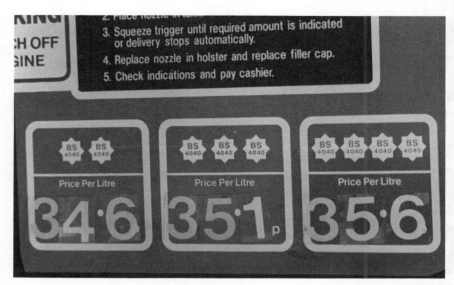

Figure 71   Petrol pump star symbols.

3) Care labels

The International Textile Care Codes (ITCC) system of labelling clothes with washing instructions has been agreed between Britain and many other countries. (See figures 72 and 73, on the next page.)

Nearly every item of clothing you buy will have a sewn-in label telling you exactly how to wash and dry or dry clean, and iron.

Fabrics are often made to imitate pure wool. When you see the label in figure 74 (page 111) you will know that garments or fabrics have been made from pure new wool.

Clothes, belts, or bags with the symbol in figure 75 (page 111) will be made of real leather.

4) Safety and quality labels

The British Standards Institution (BSI) tests a wide variety of goods sent to them by manufacturers.

If you see a Kitemark (figure 26, on page 51) on an article you will know that it is hard wearing, of good quality, and safe.

Some items will have a British Standards number without the Kitemark. This means that the product meets the British Standards, but has not been tested by BSI and so does not qualify for the mark.

(a)

	MACHINE	HAND WASH	
1 95°	Very hot to boil maximum wash	Hand-hot or boil	White cotton and linen articles without special finishes
	Spin or wring		

	MACHINE	HAND WASH	
2 60°	Hot maximum wash	Hand-hot	Cotton, linen or viscose articles without special finishes where colours are fast at 60°C
	Spin or wring		

	MACHINE	HAND WASH	
3 60°	Hot medium wash	Hand-hot	White nylon; white polyester/cotton mixtures
	Cold rinse. Short spin or drip-dry		

	MACHINE	HAND WASH	
4 50°	Hand-hot medium wash	Hand-hot	Coloured nylon; polyester; cotton and viscose articles with special finishes; acrylic/cotton mixtures; coloured polyester/cotton mixtures
	Cold rinse. Short spin or drip dry		

	MACHINE	HAND WASH	
5 40°	Warm maximum wash	Warm	Cotton, linen or viscose articles where colours are fast at 40°C, but not at 60°C
	Spin or wring		

	MACHINE	HAND WASH	
6 40°	Warm minimum wash	Warm	Acrylics; acetate and triacetate, including mixtures with wool; polyester/wool blends
	Cold rinse. Short spin. Do not wring		

	MACHINE	HAND WASH	
7 40°	Warm minimum wash	Warm Do not rub	Wool, including blankets and wool mixtures with cotton or viscose; silk
	Spin. Do not hand wring		

	MACHINE	HAND WASH	
8 30°	Cool minimum wash	Cool	Silk and printed acetate fabrics with colours not fast at 40°C
	Cold rinse. Short spin. Do not wring		

	MACHINE	HAND WASH	
9 95°	Very hot to boil minimum wash	Hand-hot or boil	Cotton articles with special finishes capable of being boiled but requiring drip drying
	Drip-dry		

	HAND WASH	
		Articles which must be machine washed. Details will vary because garment manufacturers are free to put their own written instructions on this label

 Do not wash

(b)

CHLORINE BLEACH MAY BE USED

DO NOT USE CHLORINE BLEACH

(c)

MAY BE TUMBLE DRIED

DO NOT TUMBLE DRY

(d)

WARM IRON
An iron with one dot (.) means cool
An iron with three dots (...) means hot

DO NOT IRON

(e)

MAY BE DRY CLEANED
The circle may contain letters A, P or F, depending on the requirements or limitations of the article itself. If the circle has a bar beneath it special treatment is required and advice should be sought from a professional dry cleaner.

DO NOT DRY CLEAN

Figure 72   The International Textile Care Codes.
   (a) Washing instructions.
   (b) Bleaching instructions.
   (c) Drying instructions.
   (d) Ironing instructions.
   (e) Dry cleaning instructions.

95 | White cotton and linen articles without special finishes

60 | Cotton, linen or viscose articles without special finishes where colours are fast at 60°C

60 | (Not used in UK) White nylon and white polyester/cotton mixtures are included in 50

50 | Nylon; polyester/cotton mixtures; polyester cotton and viscose articles with special finishes; cotton/acrylic mixtures

40 | Cotton, linen or viscose articles, where colours are fast at 40°C but not at 60°C

40 | Acrylics, acetate and triacetate, including mixtures with wool; polyester/wool blends

40 | Wool, wool mixed with other fibres; silk

30 | (Not used in UK) See items included in 40 and 40

95 | (Not applicable in UK)

Handwash (Do not machine wash)

Do not wash

Figure 73   These simplified wash tub symbols will be found on care labels from autumn 1987.

CERTIFICATION TRADE MARK

PURE NEW WOOL

Figure 74

real leather

Figure 75

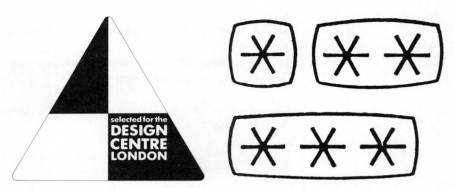

Figure 76   Design centre label.   Figure 77   Star labelling for refrigerators.

Figure 78   Freezer
symbol

The label in figure 76 shows that the product has been chosen by the Design Council as being well-made, pleasant to look at, and suitable for its job.

The star labelling for refrigerators (figure 77) shows how long frozen food may be kept in the frozen food storage compartment of the refrigerator.

The freezer symbol (figure 78) shows that a freezer can freeze fresh food as well as storing it.

The BEAB symbols in figure 25, on page 50, can be found on household electrical appliances such as kettles, food mixers, and hair dryers to show that a sample has been tested by the British Electrotechnical Approvals Board for safety, or tested by another authority and approved by BEAB.

The label in figure 79 may be found on gas appliances such as cookers and gas fires as a mark of safety and quality.

The paraffin symbol (figure 80) can be seen in shops which sell

Figure 79   BSI safety mark.

PARAFFIN

BS 2869C1

Figure 80   Paraffin symbol.

Figure 81

NHBC

Figure 82

paraffin or kerosine which is suitable for use in paraffin heaters.

The CORGI symbol (figure 81) shows that a firm is registered with the Confederation for the Registration of Gas Installers to work on gas installations. List of CORGI registered installers can be found in gas region showrooms.

The British Gas symbol (figure 55, on page 86) can be found on gas appliances which have passed British Gas standards for performance, reliability, and suitability for the job.

Figure 82 is a symbol for the National House-Building Council. Builders who use this sign agree to build their houses to standards for safety, insulation, and sound structure. The houses carry a warranty for ten years against structural faults.

Activities

Arrange a quiz to test your knowledge of these symbols.

Look at the food labels you have collected. Read the list of ingredients to your group without identifying the foods and ask them to guess what the product is..

Invent a label for something you have made yourself, *e.g.* a recipe you have made, a garment, something made from wood, paper, metal, or plastic.

SEE ALSO

Consumer information for more about where to find out about things.
Consumer protection for what to do if the things you buy go wrong.
Shopping for information about buying things.
Paying for goods for more about bar codes.

For more on food allergies and food labelling see the book *Food for Health* (in this series).

For more on food labelling see *Eat to live*, Dodie Roe, Longman, 1983.

For more on food additives see *E for additives*, Hanssen, Thorsons, 1984.

See the film "Alice in Label Land" from Concord Films Council Ltd (address on page 180).

If possible arrange a visit to the British Standards Institution or the Design Centre (addresses on page 180).

Invite someone from the Trading Standards Department or from a local shop to talk about labelling.

Lighting

Natural light is the best form of light to live and to work in. It is more restful to the eyes, and makes us feel better, but it is not always possible to have it.

Activities

Some of the different forms of lighting you may find are shown in figures 83 and 84, below and on the next page.

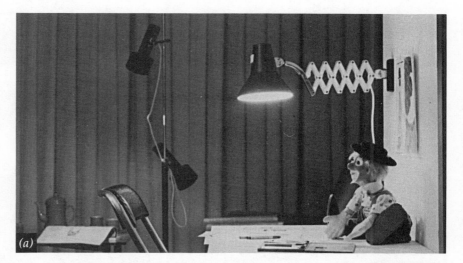

(a)

(b)

(c)

Figure 83

Figure 84

Which would send light downwards so that you could read easily?
Which would reflect light upwards onto the ceiling or walls and be suitable for background lighting in a hall?
Which might be used to give extra light in a dark corner?
Which could be used over a dining table?
Which could be used to spotlight a special picture or plant?
Which would give even light for working in a kitchen?
Which could provide night lighting for a young child's bedroom?

Look at the lighting used around your school, at home, and in shops. Which lighting gives a warm friendly glow? Which is cold and makes you look paler than you are? Where do you feel that your eyes are strained because of low lighting?

Flashing lights or strobe lighting, such as those used in discos, can make your eyes ache because the eye is continually adjusting to the changes in intensity. Eyes are more relaxed in even lighting.

Decor can affect the light in a room as well as artificial lighting. Light colours reflect light and make rooms appear larger.

Activity

If you lived in a Victorian terraced house with small dark rooms, how could you make the rooms appear lighter and larger by using:
a) artificial light
b) use of colour
c) furnishings?

SEE ALSO

Energy saving for ways of saving fuel.

Try to visit a lighting shop to look at the different alternatives you can buy.

Mortgages

A home is probably the most expensive thing most people will ever buy. Few people are able to buy a house or flat outright. It is possible to borrow the money needed, for example from a building society or bank, an insurance company, or the council. The loan on a home is called a mortgage.

Building societies

Building societies work by using the money which people invest (save) with them to lend to other people to buy a home. If you save with a building society your money will earn interest for you. If you borrow money to buy a home you will have to pay interest.

How much can you borrow?

Building societies usually lend a person $2\frac{1}{2}$ times their income. Someone earning £8000 a year could borrow about £20,000. Most building societies will take a partner's earnings into consideration too, but you should always think about the possibility of one partner giving up work at some time in the future. Don't overborrow.

Some building societies prefer you to have saved money with them if you want a loan.

They will expect you to pay a certain amount of the cost of the house in advance. This amount is called the **deposit**.

Whoever lends you the money to buy a home is called a **mortgagee**. The mortgagee will hold the deeds to your home until the money is repaid. The person borrowing the money is called the **mortgager**.

Arranging the loan

The building society, or whoever is lending you the money, will ask a number of questions. How much is the total income coming into the home? How long have you held your present job? Have you a bank account? Can you supply references? A referee is someone who will write and tell the society that you are a reliable person.

They will check the condition of the building. You will have to pay for this survey (about £50, but it depends on the cost of the home). Some societies will give you a copy of the report, but this varies. It is a very basic survey and it is wise to pay for your own detailed survey as well. This could show up things like rot in floorboards or damp in an attic, that you might not spot yourself. If you buy a new home covered by the National House-Building Council you may not need this survey.

If your loan is agreed, the legal process of buying a home starts. Most people pay a solicitor to deal with this, but some people do it themselves and the Consumers' Association publishes a booklet called *The legal side to buying a house*, which is a useful guide for this. The solicitor will carry out searches. This means that they will go to the local council and find if there are any changes planned which could affect the value of the home.

Discussion

What are some of the things which might affect the value of the home?

A home is not sold until written contracts have been exchanged between the seller (vendor) and the buyer. Once the contracts have been exchanged you cannot withdraw from buying the home – even if the buyer or seller dies, or the property is burnt down. You must therefore insure the property from the date on which the contracts are exchanged.

Activity

Find out how much interest you get on money saved with a building society, and how much interest you will pay on a loan.
Who could you ask to write a reference for the building society?

SEE ALSO

Homes for information about choosing homes.
Insurance for more about how and when to insure your home.
Rates to find out about services provided by the local authority.
Labelling for more about the National House-Building Council.

Invite someone from a local building society to explain about the different methods of paying a mortgage and how to obtain tax relief – MIRAS (mortgage interest relief at source).

Paying for goods

When you buy items which cost a lot of money you may have the chance of paying:

by cash
by cheque
by credit card
by electronic fund transfer
by credit (paying over a period of time, for example by hire
   purchase)
by standing order.

Paying by cash

If you have enough money you can pay outright by cash. Be careful, though, when carrying large sums of money around. Some firms, for example those supplying double glazing or bedroom fittings, will charge less if a cash payment is made, so it is worth asking.

Paying by cheque

If you have a bank account you can pay for goods by writing a cheque. Most shops will insist on a cheque card or some other form of identification. A cheque card can be obtained from your bank and will guarantee that amounts up to £50 will be paid by the bank. A cheque and cheque guarantee card are shown in figure 85.

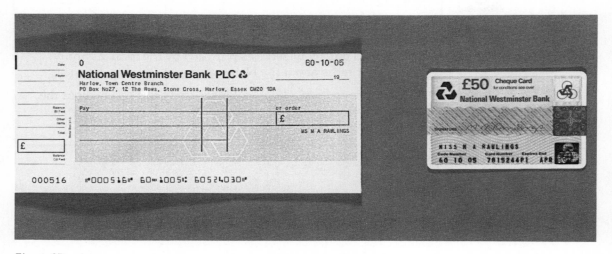

Figure 85

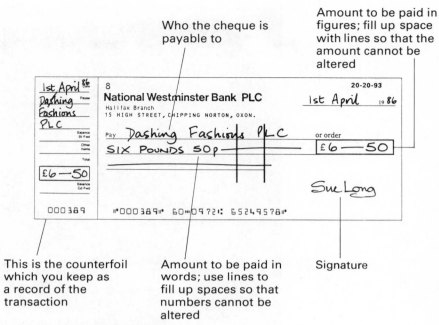

Who the cheque is
payable to

Amount to be paid in
figures; fill up space
with lines so that the
amount cannot be
altered

This is the counterfoil
which you keep as
a record of the
transaction

Amount to be paid in
words; use lines to
fill up spaces so that
numbers cannot be
altered

Signature

Figure 86   How to fill in a cheque.

Figure 86 shows you how to fill in a cheque.

A cheque card is sometimes a cash card too, which means that it can
also be used to obtain sums of money, from your bank account, from a
cash dispenser outside the bank. This is useful when the bank has
closed. Other banks have separate cash and cheque cards. When you
get a cash card from the bank you are given a PIN (personal
identification number), and you have to type this number into the cash
dispenser to get money out (figure 87). Cash dispensers can also tell
you how much money you have in your account. Some cash
dispensers also let you pay money in.

You can also have a bank account with the post office. This is called
the National Girobank. You get a cheque book and can have a cheque
card to write cheques to pay for goods as well as for drawing money at
two post offices (perhaps your local post office and one near work).
Post offices open longer hours than banks, and on Saturday mornings
so can be more convenient. However with a bank you can use any of
its branches, and are not limited to just two.

Paying by credit card

Figure 88 shows two different credit cards. They can be used to pay for
goods. You are given a credit limit – an amount up to which you may
spend when you first get a card – and this amount is raised from time
to time if you use the card properly. You give your cheque card to the
shop assistant who makes out a payment slip which you have to sign.

Figure 87   Cash dispenser.

If the amount is large the assistant may ring up and check that it is not more than your credit limit.

At the end of the month the bill for the goods arrives. If you pay within the stated time limit you do not have to pay any interest, but if you delay paying you start to pay interest on the amount owing.

You can have a Barclaycard even if you do not have a bank account at Barclays Bank, and it can be used for withdrawing money from a cash dispenser too, but you start paying interest on this money immediately.

Cash and credit cards should be kept somewhere safe and not with your cheque book, and your PIN should be kept secret. Do not write it down where anyone who finds or steals the card may find it. If you do lose your card, or it is stolen you must inform the credit card company immediately. If you do not you will be liable for the bills the other person runs up.

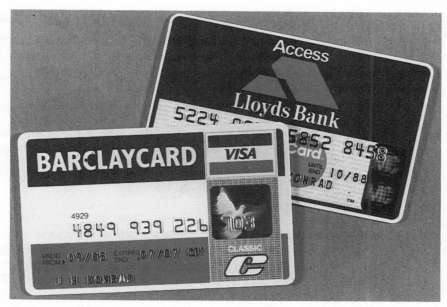

Figure 88   Credit cards.

Electronic fund transfer (EFT)

In some shops you can use your cash card to pay for goods and the money is immediately withdrawn from your bank account. The shop has a computer connected to the computer at your bank. You give the shop assistant your cash card, and you key your PIN into a machine. The magnetic strip on the card is read by the computer and the amount of money is taken from your account and transferred automatically into the shop's account.

Shops say that EFT will make paying for goods faster than writing cheques or using credit cards, and we won't have to carry money around with us. But think what would happen in these situations:

Discussion/Activity

There is a long queue of people at the check-out on a busy Saturday. The EFT system rejects your card even though you know you have money in your account.

Someone pays for something by EFT, but instead of the computer taking the money from their account it is taken from yours.

A small shop installs EFT, but has to put up prices to cover the cost of the expensive equipment.

Write a letter to your local paper about the installation of EFT into shops in your area. You may be either for or against EFT.

Bar codes

You may have noticed on many things you buy that there is a series of black lines, like the one in figure 69 on page 108. This is a bar code, and eventually most goods sold in shops will be bar coded.

A bar code is made up of a 13-digit number. The black lines and spaces are the numbers in a form readable by a computer.

The first two digits tell you which country the number comes from; the United Kingdom code is 50. The next five digits show who the manufacturer is, the next five the product, and the last digit is a check digit to make sure that the code is correct. Every product and each variation in size, colour, etc. has to have a different number.

At the check-out instead of ringing the prices up on a till the assistant will pass the bar code over a laser scanner which will read the bar code. The store computer will send the price of that item to the check-out. It will appear on a display panel at the desk and will be printed on the receipt (figure 89).

```
                                    £
        S-R WHLML FLOUR        0.59
        BATH CLEANER           0.95
        PRODUCE                0.39

    AUBERGINES
    1.30 lb @    £0.78/lb      1.01
    PEACHES
          2 @    £0.18         0.36
        CARROTS                0.24

    52 BAL DUE                30.39

    CHEQUE                    30.39
    CHANGE                     0.00
```

Figure 89

As the computer gives the price to the check-out the assistant will not have to read the price on each item. Shops will probably stop putting price labels on every item and just put them on the shelf edge instead.

As well as informing the assistant of the price the computer will register that an item has been sold and when stocks get to a certain level may warn that reordering is necessary.

Discussion

What will happen when the shop wants to put up prices?

How will you check that shelf prices match till prices?

What happens when shoppers or assistants put goods back on the wrong shelf?

How will you make sure that you are paying the right amount for goods?

Paying by standing order

When you have to pay for something regularly, like electricity or the repayments for a hire purchase agreement, you can arrange for the bank to do this for you from your bank account (or from your National Girobank account).

You tell the bank how much is to be paid and the date on which it is to be paid, and the money will be transferred direct from your bank account to the account of the person receiving the money.

SEE ALSO

Credit for more about paying over a period of time.

Rates

 Collect a copy of the rates precept from your local council offices or town hall.

Every householder has to pay rates to the local authority. If you live in rented accommodation this may be included with the rent. If you own your own home you will have to pay rates as well as a mortgage.

Rates are used to pay for services which everyone in an area uses, for example:

collecting rubbish
mending roads
providing schools
providing facilities, for example leisure facilities, libraries, swimming pools, youth clubs, parks, the fire service, the police.

Activity

From the rates precept find out how each pound in the rates is spent. Which services are most expensive?

How much do you pay?

The amount of rates you pay depends on the rateable value of your home. The more amenities your home has, for example a garden, garage, central heating, many rooms, etc, the more rates you pay. They do not depend on the number of people living in a home. Rates are assessed as so much in the pound. If in one year the rates are 80 p in the pound and the rateable value of your house is £200, your yearly rates bill will be:

£200 × 0.80 p =   (Fill in the answer)

Rates are usually paid each half year, but you can arrange to pay each month if you prefer.

Water rates

All householders pay a water rate as well as the general rate. This covers the water supply to the home and the treatment of waste (sewage).

Discussion/Activity

Do you think the rating system is fair?

Can you think of any other system for paying rates?

If you were in charge of allocating the money collected from the rates, how would you do it?

Draw a plan of your town centre. Mark all the places paid for with money from the rates.

Refrigerators

Collect manufacturers' leaflets for refrigerators; a recent *Which?* report on refrigerators.

Figure 90   (a) Small refrigerator.
(b) Larder refrigerator.

Storing food in a refrigerator will mean that you can keep it for longer. It won't be necessary to shop as often, and any leftover food may be saved. The refrigerator can also be used for making ice cubes, setting jellies, and storing frozen foods.

Activities

Look at the refrigerator in the Home Economics room or at home and answer the following questions:

1) What size (in cubic feet or litres) is it? You may have to look at the booklet supplied with the refrigerator to find this out. You should allow at least one cubic foot for each member of the family when buying a refrigerator. Think also about any special needs of

members of the family, for example extra space for milk for a baby.

2) Is it gas or electric?

3) Find a similar model in one of the leaflets. How much does it cost?

4) On a copy of figure 91 show:

the freezing compartment or evaporator
door storage
shelves
salad drawer

for your refrigerator.

Figure 91

5) Are the shelves easily removable?

6) How long may frozen foods be kept in this refrigerator? You will need to look at the star markings to find out.

    * = one week

   ** = one month

*** = three months

   Compartments which are not marked with stars are only suitable for making ice cubes. Some refrigerators have no ice-making compartment. They are known as larder fridges.

7) Does it have a right- or left-hand opening door?

8) Does it have a light inside?

9) What type of defrosting does it have

a) manual

b) automatic

c) semi-automatic?

These are the sorts of questions you should be asking when looking for a refrigerator to buy.

Look at your *Which?* report on refrigerators. What does *Which?* suggest that you should consider when buying a refrigerator?

Where would you buy a refrigerator?

There are several places where you can buy refrigerators:
Electricity or Gas Board showrooms
electrical shops
chain stores
discount warehouses.

Activity

Choose one make of refrigerator and cost it at each of the above places. List your costs in order.

How cold is it in a refrigerator?

Activity

Answer these questions, using figure 92:
At what temperatures does a refrigerator operate?
At what temperature would you make ice?
At what temperature are frozen foods stored in the refrigerator?

Storage in the refrigerator

Cold air is heavy and falls. This is why the evaporator is at the top of the refrigerator. As the cold air falls it collects warmth and moisture from foods. This warmer air then rises because it is lighter. The moisture condenses and becomes frozen on the evaporator.

Some refrigerators, now, are frost-free. The moisture is either led into a box which has to be emptied or it is evaporated by the condenser into the air.

Activity

Show with a star on a copy of your refrigerator diagram where you will store the foods which need the coldest conditions.

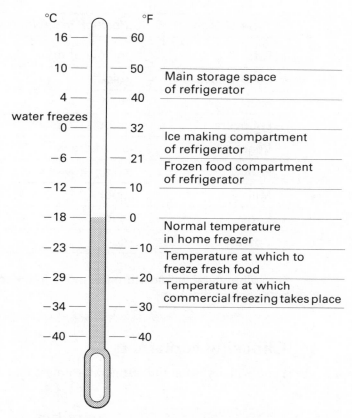

Figure 92   Temperature conversion chart.

Larder refrigerators (see figure 90b) do not have a frozen food compartment. They are ideal for people who already have a freezer.

Activity

Type of food	Position in cabinet	Length of time
Ice cubes	evaporator	2–3 months
Frozen foods	evaporator	according to stars
Meat	high	joint 4–5 days mince 1–3 days poultry 2–3 days bacon 7–10 days
Cheese	middle	hard 30 days cottage 1 week

Type of food	Position in cabinet	Length of time
Fats	middle or door	3–7 days
Sandwiches	middle	24 hours
Fish	high	1–2 days
Leftovers	middle	2–3 days
Vegetables	salad drawer	3–7 days
Fruit	salad drawer	1–3 days
Milk	door	3 days
Eggs	door	2 weeks
Bottles	door	varies

Show how you would store the foods in the table above on your refrigerator diagram.

Choosing containers

Food will dry up in the refrigerator unless it is covered.

Activities

Try this experiment to see which is the best material for keeping food fresh and crisp in the refrigerator.

You will need
  a packet of ice cream wafers
  bags and containers, *e.g.* polythene bags, foil wrap, clingfilm,
    plastic container, covered dish, greaseproof paper, paper bag
  cobalt chloride papers

1) Cut cobalt chloride papers in strips 2 × 8 cm. Dry, for example over the heat of the radiator. The strips should turn blue.
2) Put an ice cream wafer in each container with a cobalt chloride strip. Seal with sticky tape.
3) The cobalt chloride paper will turn pink if there is moisture.
4) Leave for a few days in the fridge, then look at the strips.
5) The pink strips will show the containers which will keep foods freshest.

Make a list of the foods in the table on pages 131 and 132. By the side of each write how you would pack them for the refrigerator.

Defrosting

Activity

Find out from a refrigerator booklet how to defrost the refrigerator. Write clear instructions for how to do this. Give the instructions to someone else to follow. Did they have any problems?

Some refrigerators will defrost automatically.

SEE ALSO

Freezers to find out how to keep foods for long periods of time.

Responsibilities

Collect some of the DHSS leaflets shown in figure 93.

Do you have anyone or anything that you are responsible for? Perhaps you are responsible for looking after a family pet, cleaning out your own room, or baby-sitting for younger brothers and sisters. Do you enjoy this or regard it as a chore?

If a family is to live happily together each member of the family group must take a share in the responsibilities of the home. It can lead to family friction if one member of the family thinks he or she is doing all the work.

Discussion

What chain of events do you think might have led up to the following?

"It's not fair. I always do the washing-up and you let David get on with his homework and then go out with his friends."

"You think I'm just the drudge in this house. I've been slaving away all day cooking and cleaning and now you expect me to iron your shirt."

Is it right that the same person always does the same household jobs?

Who would you expect to do the following in the home:

hoovering
cooking
regular cleaning of the whole house
dusting
washing
walking the dog
cleaning shoes

washing-up
making beds
cleaning the car
mending clothes
cleaning the bath
painting and decorating
ironing?

How could a family with two adults and children aged 10 and 15 share out these jobs in the home?

Being a member of a family also means being willing to consider the needs of others.

Discussion

What are the difficulties that may occur when young people and old live in the same house?

What changes may a new baby in the family bring?

What are the problems which may be faced when one member of the family is handicapped?

Financial help

The State has taken responsibility for the provision of financial help for people at particular times in their lives, when they need it. The cost of these services is met through the taxes we pay and through the National Insurance contributions paid by employed people.

Figure 93   Selection of DHSS leaflets.

You need to contact your local branch of the Department of Health and Social Security if you think you are eligible for any of the benefits shown in the leaflets in figure 93. The rates for these benefits frequently change, and it is necessary to obtain up-to-date leaflets when aid is required.

Here are some examples.

Unemployment Benefit

This is payable if you are unemployed and available to work for an employer. If you have worked before and paid enough National Insurance contributions a standard rate is paid which can be increased by an addition for an adult dependant.

Supplementary Benefit

You may be entitled to this if you are not in full-time work and your income is below a certain level. If you receive Supplementary Benefit you are also entitled to other benefits such as free dental treatment, free NHS vouchers for glasses, free NHS prescriptions, etc.

Child Benefit

This is a cash sum payable for all children in the family. It is normally paid every four weeks in arrears. An extra amount is paid to one-parent families.

Family Income Supplement

This is paid to families where the man or woman is in full-time work, where there is at least one child in the family and the total income is below a certain amount. If you are entitled to Family Income Supplement you are also entitled to:

free milk and vitamins for expectant mothers and children under
  school age;
free school meals;
free NHS prescriptions, dental treatment, and vouchers for
  glasses;
refund of fares to and from hospital;
free legal advice (legal aid).

Sickness Benefit

This is paid if you cannot work through ill health. Where you have an employer you will usually receive Statutory Sick Pay instead. After 28 weeks you are paid "invalidity" benefit in its place.

Retirement Pension

This is paid to men over 65 and woman over 60 who have retired from work. Depending on the area they live in, people on retirement pension can also be entitled to benefits such as cheap bus fares.

Statutory Maternity Pay

From April 1987 Statutory Maternity Pay (SMP) replaced maternity allowance and is paid by employers for a maximum of 18 weeks subject to an employment condition. A woman who does not qualify may be entitled to a weekly maternity allowance from the DHSS. To qualify, she must have been employed and paid full National Insurance contributions before the baby was born. From the same date, maternity payment from the Social Fund replaced maternity grant and Supplementary Benefit.

Single payments for maternity needs: Maternity payments are payable to people receiving Supplementary Benefit or Family Income Supplement. Savings over £500 are offset against the amount payable.

Widow's Benefit

This is paid to a woman when her husband dies. It is not paid to a man when his wife dies.

Do you think this is fair? What is the reasoning behind it?

Attendance Allowance

This is paid to those who are mentally or physically disabled and need looking after.

Invalid Care Allowance

This is paid to people who stay at home to look after disabled relatives instead of working.

Mobility Allowance

This is a weekly cash benefit to which you may be entitled if you are unable or virtually unable to walk through physical disablement and are likely to remain so for at least a year.

Death Grant/Funeral Payment

As from 6 April 1987 the "death grant" has been abolished and replaced by a "funeral payment" from the Social Fund. Those with savings of more than £500 will be expected to use the excess towards the cost of the funeral. However, anyone in receipt of Supplementary Benefit, Family Income Supplement or Housing Benefit will automatically qualify for help towards the funeral expenses.

Activity

Some DHSS leaflets are not very easy to read. Chose one of your DHSS leaflets and study it carefully. Try to explain to someone else what benefits are available and how you set about getting them.

Try filling in any forms which are provided. Make a list of any words you do not understand.

Self-help groups and voluntary organisations

Voluntary organisations are groups of people who feel they have a responsibility to help those who need it. They are not paid, but get satisfaction from feeling that they have been of use. Self-help groups are groups of people with similar problems who meet to provide help and support for each other. They don't have nationally recognised names like the voluntary organisations but vary from area to area.

The Citizens Advice Bureau and local newspapers will be able to provide information about any groups that meet in your area.

Here are some of the voluntary organisations you might find in your area.

The Samaritans

The Samaritans provide someone at the end of a telephone line to talk to if you feel unhappy or upset. You do not have to give your name and all calls are treated in confidence; but they will arrange to meet you if that is what you want. Their address and telephone number will be in the telephone book.

Gingerbread

Gingerbread brings one-parent families together. They arrange meetings, outings, and holidays at low cost.

National Council for One-Parent Families

This organisation helps single parents (widowed, single, separated, or divorced) and their children by giving advice about housing, jobs, nursery care, adoption, and legal advice.

WRVS

The Women's Royal Voluntary Service provides mother and baby groups, senior citizens' groups, play centres, meals on wheels, visitors for those in prison or hospital.

Marriage Guidance Council

The Marriage Guidance Council helps couples who are having problems in their relationships.

British Red Cross Society

The Red Cross provides first aid at events, and organises holidays for the elderly and disabled. They also run hospital canteens and visit hospital patients.

Age Concern

Age Concern provides lunch-clubs and meetings for elderly people. They organise chiropody and hairdressing sessions.

Activity

Look in your local newspaper and find out the organisations which exist in your area. Which sections of the population are they for?

  Are there any sections of the population who may need help, but are not being catered for? Self-help groups are set up to fill gaps like this.

SEE ALSO

For more information about welfare services during pregnancy or for young children see the book *Families and Child Development* (in this series).

You may be able to arrange for someone from the Citizens Advice Bureau or WRVS to come and talk to you about the work they are doing. You may also be able to offer time to a voluntary organisation to help.

Safety

Collect cuttings from the national or local newspapers reporting accidents in the home or garden or on the road.
OR
Carry out a survey of accidents that have happened to you, or to younger brothers or sisters. Write these up like the reports in the newspapers.

Activity

For each of your reports decide whether the accident was the fault of:

the victim
someone else who was present
a faulty appliance
poor labelling or instructions
any other factors.

How could each of these accidents have been prevented?

Who has accidents?

Information is collected from people who attend hospital as the result of an accident in the home. A poster in the hospital will ask you take part in the Home Accident Surveillance System's survey (HASS). The information is used by the government's Consumer Safety Unit at the Department of Prices and Consumer Protection to find out the answers to questions like these:

Are people of certain ages more likely to have accidents?
Do certain products cause accidents?
Which are the commonest injuries?

How does knowing the answer to these sort of questions help:

the government
your family
you?

When someone dies unexpectedly an inquest (a special kind of enquiry) is held by the local coroner. Coroners supply details of accidental deaths to the government. The table below shows deaths caused by accidents during the last three months of one year.

ACCIDENTAL DEATHS IN THE HOME, 1983

Type of injury	0–4	5–14	15–64	65–74	75 and over	Total
			Age (years)			
Fracture	18	2	254	302	1,823	2,399
Poisoning/suspected poisoning	6	8	405	60	58	537
Suffocation	65	42	173	47	114	441
Burn/scald	28	10	109	61	141	349
Foreign body	24	3	125	53	84	289
Concussion	8	1	61	50	137	257
Cut/laceration/open wound	11	3	44	18	57	133
Other internal injury	4	3	49	15	42	113
Dislocation	0	1	4	2	11	18
Bruise/contusion	0	0	1	0	8	9
Ingestion	0	0	3	1	2	6
Sprain/strain	0	0	1	2	2	5
Other	47	25	157	71	144	445
Unknown	3	3	18	13	17	54
Total	214	101	1,404	695	2,641	5,055

Activity

Find out from the table:
1) What is the most common cause of accidental death?
2) What is the most common danger to elderly people?
3) What is the most common danger to under five-year-olds?
4) What is the most common danger to your age group?

Where do accidents happen?

In the home

The table on the next page was produced as a result of a HASS survey. It shows where accidents happened in the home during the first year of the survey.

Activities

1) Which are the most dangerous places in the house?
2) Which are the most dangerous places for your age group?

WHERE ACCIDENTS HAPPEN (FIGURES FOR 1983)

Place	Age (years)						
	0–4	5–14	15–64	65–74	75 and over	Unknown	Total
Living/dining room	5,815	2,075	4,165	517	843	23	13,438
Kitchen	2,691	1,222	7,624	772	677	25	13,011
Garden/grassed area	2,015	2,486	4,068	549	359	5	9,482
Inside stairs	1,594	1,007	4,009	398	431	10	7,449
Bedroom	1,933	1,270	2,172	270	845	10	6,500
Yard/driveway/path	937	988	2,760	300	270	3	5,258
Bathroom/toilet	657	318	1,119	174	305	6	2,579
Hall/lobby	678	304	816	99	205	1	2,103
Garage/garden shed	134	264	1,464	123	39	3	2,027
Outside stairs/steps	359	154	732	121	124	4	1,494
Porch/threshold	296	275	696	94	83	1	1,445
Landing	131	104	360	23	28	0	646
Balcony/patio	93	57	212	20	11	0	393
Loft/attic	8	21	110	3	4	0	146
Cellar	7	8	43	3	3	1	65
Other	160	176	434	47	58	2	877
Unknown	10,517	6,080	20,677	2,259	3,697	111	43,341
Total	28,025	16,809	51,461	5,772	7,982	205	110,245

The ten objects in figure 94 are the most common causes of accidents in the home.

What sort of accidents do you think they cause?

In the garden

Activity

List ten things which might cause accidents in the garden; for example, young children playing and gardeners using electricity.

On the road

Activity

On the road you may come across the signs in figure 95. They warn of danger.

Match the signs up with their meanings.

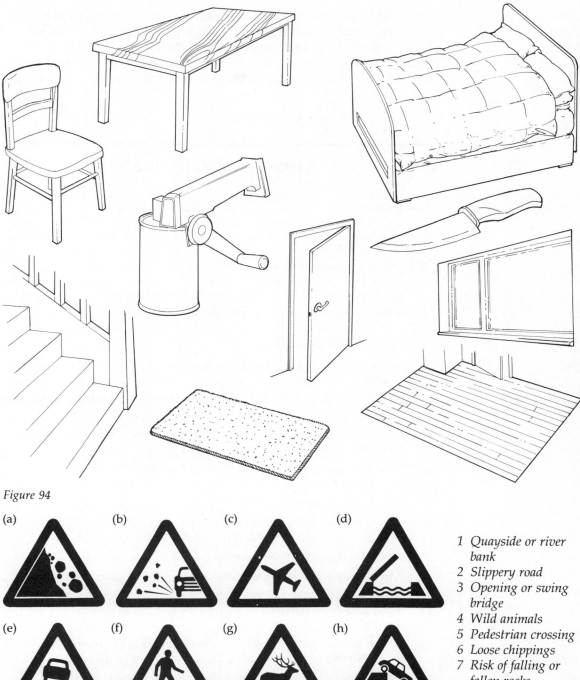

Figure 94

(a)   (b)   (c)   (d)

(e)   (f)   (g)   (h)

Figure 95

1 Quayside or river bank
2 Slippery road
3 Opening or swing bridge
4 Wild animals
5 Pedestrian crossing
6 Loose chippings
7 Risk of falling or fallen rocks
8 Low-flying aircraft or sudden aircraft noise

So many people were killed going through the windscreen of a car in an accident that there is now a law which makes the wearing of seat belts, in the front of a car, compulsory. This is one example of legislation (law-enforcement) for safety. In many other situations it is up to the individuals to decide for themselves what is safe and what is not.

What can **you** do about safety?

EMERGENCY CHECKLIST

Your name ....
Your address ....
....

1. Who is your doctor? ....

2. Where is his surgery? (address) ....
....
.... (telephone number) ....

3. Where is your nearest hospital with a casualty department? ....
....

4. Where is your nearest chemist? ....

5. Where do you keep first aid things at home? ....
....

6. What is the emergency telephone number of the ambulance and fire brigade? ....

7. If you live in a flat, what is the telephone number of the porter or service engineer? ....

8. Where do you turn off the electricity in your home? ....
....

9. Where is the fuse box in your home? ....

10. Where do you keep a) spare fuses? ....
                            b) fuse wire? ....

11. Where do you turn off the water? ....

12. Where and how do you turn off the main supply of gas in your home? .....
....

13. If you smell gas, what is the emergency telephone number of your Gas Region? ....

14. Where can you get in touch with your Mum, Dad or other close relative during the day? ....

15. Where is the public telephone call box nearest to your home? ....

Figure 96

Activities

Fill in the form in figure 96. This is information you may need in the event of an accident.

Find out where the places you might need in an emergency are.
    Draw a map of your town centre and fill in as many of these on it as you can:

hospital	Citizens Advice Bureau
police station	Gas and Electricity Board
fire station	showrooms
Consumer Advice Centre	town hall or council offices

    Also mark the things which may help to save accidents, for example pedestrian crossings, traffic lights, roundabouts, safety barriers, play areas, warning signs.

Draw a plan of your kitchen, bedroom, and living room. Mark on it the safety features you have thought about to make these safe rooms to be in.

How others can help

Warning signs or labels can help prevent accidents.
    The signs in figures 97, 98, and 99 are meant to be international – they can be read in any language.
    Figure 97 shows **don't** signs. What do they mean?
    Figure 98 shows **watch out** signs. What is the danger?
    Figure 99 shows **do** signs, used mainly in industry. What are they telling you to do?

Activity

Make up similar signs for the following:

silence
broken glass
poisonous snakes.

Show the signs to four other people. Can they understand what they mean?

Figure 97   DON'T signs.

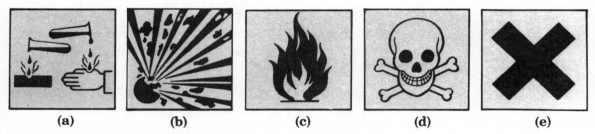

Figure 98   WATCH OUT signs.

Figure 99   DO signs.

Laws about safety

These are laws which have been passed to make sure that some safety precautions are carried out.

Consumer Protection Act (amended 1971)

This law lets the Secretary of State make regulations about products if it is necessary. For example if a new product comes onto the market and it is thought to be unsafe, then the act can be used to stop the sale of the product. There are regulations about things such as oil heaters, nightdresses, electric blankets, make-up, etc. Any product which you think is unsafe should be taken to the Trading Standards Officer, who will follow up the complaint for you.

The regulations under this act apply also to second-hand goods, but not to goods sold privately. This means that most local jumble sales count as private sales.

Consumer Safety Act

See page 29.

Health and Safety Act (1974)

This act aims to:
Provide for health, safety, and welfare of people at work.
Protect other people against risks to health or safety caused at work.
It also covers schools.

Explosives Act (1976)

Makes it an offence to sell fireworks to people under 16 years of age, and to throw fireworks in the street.

Food and Drugs Act (1955)

See page 29.

Home Safety Act

This act allows the Home Safety Officers to visit schools and clubs to talk about safety.

Medicines Act (1968)

This act says that certain medicines must be sold in child-proof containers, and that other poisonous medicines must be sold in bottles with ridges down the sides. You often see these bottles used for bleach, too.

TODDLER ALMOST HANGED IN BANNED "KILLER" COAT

A game on a garden slide almost turned into disaster for young David Sparkes – because of his "killer" coat. Three-year-old David was nearly hanged by the cord on his Hong Kong made parka.

Now his angry parents have complained to the local Council's Trading Standards Officer because they want to see neck cords on childrens' coats banned.

But last night officials of the Royal Society for the Prevention of Accidents (RoSPA) were alarmed by the case – because they say this type of coat fastener is already banned.

David's lucky escape from death happened as he played on a new slide in his parents' garden in Chase Avenue, Callow. The hood cord, which was tied, caught on the top of the slide and David tumbled over the edge. The cord tightened under his weight and left him hanging.

A spokesman for RoSPA in London said "Four years ago this type of children's anorak with hood cords was withdrawn and manufacturers were advised to use elastic instead."

"This followed a number of accidents involving children being choked – mainly from climbing railings and trees."

Figure 100

Figure 101

Figure 102

Figure 103

Activities

Figures 100 to 103 show some accounts or pictures of accidents. For each one write down or discuss:

Whose fault was the accident?
What safety precautions could have been taken?
Were there any safety or warning labels which should have been heeded?
Is there any law which should have prevented the accident?
Is there anyone who could help?
How could an accident like this be prevented in the future?
What would you have done?

Make a poster or leaflet for the following:

Safety hints for the elderly.
How to have a safe kitchen.
Safety in the garden.
Make the road a safer place to be.

SEE ALSO

Adhesives
Aerosols
Consumer protection
Electricity   } for more about safety.
Gas
Kitchen planning
Labelling for more about safety labelling.

For information on safety with young children see the book *Families and Child Development* (in this series).

Savings

Can you think of anything which you have saved to buy, rather than buying outright, either recently, or when you were younger?

People tend to save for expensive items like a holiday, a new coat, a motorbike, or the deposit for a house, or just for anything unexpected which might happen.

Depending on where you save it might be possible for your money to earn some interest, so that you end up with more than you have put away.

Ways of saving

1) Piggy bank

Figure 104

Young children are often given a piggy bank (figure 104) to start them off on saving for small items; but you can also buy one with separate compartments to save for gas, coal, or rent. It is not wise to keep large sums of money in the house in this way, though, in case of burglary.

2) Post Office

Anyone over seven can open a savings account. You have a book in which to keep a record of your savings. You can take out up to £20 on demand. You are paid interest (about 4 per cent) on your money. You can also open a deposit account with the National Girobank. Money can be paid in from a current account with the Girobank or paid direct into the deposit account. The deposit account will earn interest.

3) Trustee Savings Bank

This works in a similar way to the Post Office, but you can take out larger sums of money. They will also arrange to pay your bills for you.

4) Building societies

This is a good way of saving if you want to buy a house eventually as building societies prefer to lend money if you have saved with them regularly. You are paid interest on your money.

5) Premium bonds

These are bought in £5 units. You are not paid interest, but the bonds are put in a weekly draw, and you have the chance of winning £50–250,000.

6) Save As You Earn (SAYE)

You can arrange to have your savings taken directly from your salary, but there is a limit on the amount you can save each month. The scheme is administered by National Savings and the money invested is used by the government. Tax is not payable on these savings.

7) Bank accounts

Most banks have special accounts which earn interest for savings, for example a deposit account.

Activities

Which of these methods of saving do you think would be most suitable:

a) to save for a holiday
b) for regular saving
c) to save for the deposit on a house?

Find out the interest rates at the building society, bank and Post Office. Who offers the best interest rate?

Building societies and banks often have different savings schemes with different interest rates, amount of first deposits, total amount which can be saved, and amounts for withdrawal at long or short notice.

Activity

Choose one building society or bank and make a comparison of what they have to offer. Make a chart to show your results.

Some building societies or banks have special schemes to encourage young children to save regularly.

Activity

How would you encourage a young child to start saving?

SEE ALSO

Budgeting for ways of planning spending.

Invite someone from a building society or bank to talk to you about what they offer, especially any schemes they have to encourage young children to save regularly.

Shopping

Send for the Office of Fair Trading codes of practice (shoes, electrical goods, cars, double glazing, buying by post, package holidays, furniture, funerals, launderers and dry cleaners, photography, home improvements) and the leaflets on buying by post and how to cope with doorstep salesmen (address on page 180).

Also send for the leaflets on laser scanning, computer shopping, and paying by plastic card from the Welsh Consumer Council (address on page 180).

Who shops for what?

Discuss who in the family might shop for:

food
furniture
holidays

a refrigerator
jeans
a car

and why this might be.

Where can you shop?

Some of the ways in which we might "go shopping" today are shown in the colour section, between pages 106 and 107. Though whether we all have as much choice as this will depend on where we live – city, town, or village.

Activity

Carry out a survey of the shops in your area. How many of those shown in the colour section (between pages 106 and 107) could you use?

Find out about:

opening/closing times
facilities for the disabled (*e.g.* ramps rather than stairs)
provision for babies, young children
standards of hygiene (*e.g.* in food shops are assistants wearing protective clothing, do they use tongs for picking up unwrapped food?)

How do you choose which shops to use?

Once you know the range of shops there are in your area how will you decide which to use?

If you are shopping for food you might have the choice of a supermarket, small corner shop, market, freezer centre, or mobile shop. Which shop you choose may depend on how quickly you need the food, whether you have transport, the cost, how likely you are to be persuaded into buying other goods which you really do not need, how you could pay.

It may help to make a list of the advantages and disadvantages of each type of shopping.

Activities

What are the advantages or disadvantages of the items starred in the supermarket pictures in figure 105 (below and on the next page)?

Make a similar list or drawing for the other food shops in the colour section (between pages 106 and 107).

Figure 105   (part)

Figure 105   (continued)

If you were going to buy some furniture what would your choice of shops be where you live? List the advantages and disadvantages of these.

What are the advantages and disadvantages of armchair shopping by computer?

Write a letter to your local newspaper in support of or against:

Pedestrian areas – large shopping areas with no traffic.
Hypermarkets – large, out of town supermarket/chain stores with parking facilities.
The stopping of milk delivery to the doorstep.

How do you choose what to buy?

When you last bought something:

Was the cost the only consideration?
Did you shop around (look at the same thing in a number of shops) to compare prices, quality?
Did you find out anything about what you were going to buy by reading about it beforehand?

The kinds of booklets you could read are shown in figure 106.

Were there any labels provided on the item to give you more information about, for example, safety or laundering?
Did you think about the materials it was made of: would it last (be durable), would it wash, break, etc?
Was there a guarantee?

Your answers to these questions will depend on the object you were buying.

If you want to avoid being disappointed with your purchases you need to think ahead, rather than making impulse buys (buying things on the spur of the moment). **Thinking ahead** will help you to **spend money wisely**.

It is possible to try some things out before you buy them – you can sit on a chair or try on a pair of shoes, for example. With some goods, particularly expensive, electrical goods this is not possible. Let us

Figure 106   A selection of Office of Fair Trading booklets.

suppose you are going to buy a hair dryer.

How can you be sure you are going to spend money wisely, when you cannot try it out in advance? Here is a check-list of some of the questions you might ask yourself.

1) How much is it?

Look in the shops at the range available. Ask about them. Make a note of the prices and any differences between the different models, *i.e.* **shop around**.

2) How many speeds has it got?
3) Does it blow hot and cold?
4) How heavy is it?
5) Is it an easy shape to use?
6) Are there any extras, *e.g.* a styling nozzle, brush, comb, etc.?

7) What colour is it? Is this important?

8) Is there a guarantee?

9) Is there a BEAB label, showing that it is electrically safe?

10) Will you want to use it in other countries – if so has it got dual voltage (a small switch which will change it from the 240 volts needed in this country to 110 volts)?

11) Are there any reports or articles, *e.g.* a *Which?* report, to find out more information from?

The kind of check-list you draw up will vary depending on the item you are buying. For example with larger items the method of payment might be important – you might want to pay by credit card or hire purchase rather than cash.

Activity

Try writing a check-list for buying the following:

a pair of wellingtons for a four-year-old
a motor cycle crash helmet
a weekend holiday in Paris
a microwave cooker
a pair of jeans

Some of the leaflets mentioned at the beginning of this topic will help.

What happens if things go wrong?

Figure 107   (part)

Figure 107
(continued)

What happens if, in spite of all your care things go wrong with a
purchase – your boots let in water, the microwave light doesn't work,
your jeans split?

That is when you need to know about your rights as a consumer.

SEE ALSO

Consumer information for help when choosing goods.
Labelling for information about the labels which can help you to
make a choice.
Paying for goods for methods of payment.

A set of data files, for use with the "QUEST" information retrieval
program, concerned with the criteria for choosing electrical
equipment, is available from the Advisory Unit for Computer-
Based Education (address on page 180). The files, which are of
cookers, microwave cookers, freezers, and fridges were produced
in conjunction with the Electricity Council.

Stain removal

 Collect small samples of a variety of fabrics.

Many stains can be removed by soaking or washing with soap powders if the fabric is washable. All stains should be tackled straight away by putting into cold water (hot water will set stains), then washing.

How to treat difficult stains

If you have to try any other ways of getting a stain out put a clean cloth under the stain, and, using a cloth or sponge, dab at the stain working from the outside in towards the centre. Rinse well then wash.

Blood, milk, gravy, egg

Soak in a warm solution of biological detergent. Rinse well, then wash as usual.

Tea, coffee

Soak in hand-hot washing powder, then wash at the highest possible temperature which is recommended for the fabric.

Grass

Soak in biological detergent or sponge with methylated spirits.

Oil, grease, margarine, or butter

Soak and wash in grease-solvent washing powder, or use a grease solvent. Grease solvents (dissolvers) can be bought at the chemist or at a hardware store under trade names, *e.g.* Dabitoff. Grease solvents produce fumes which can be dangerous – only use in an airy room.

Biro

Use methylated spirits, then wash.

Chewing gum

Harden by putting in the freezer or refrigerator. Scrape off.

Unfortunately some fabrics may be damaged by these kinds of treatment.

How likely is it that you will spoil a garment trying to remove a stain?

Activity

Stain some of the fabrics you have collected with any of the stains mentioned above. Allow to dry. Try removing the stain by the method shown.
Notice:

if the stain has gone
whether any colour is left behind on the cloth
if the colour of the original fabric has changed
if the structure of the fabric has changed at all, for example threads pulled out of shape.

It would be useful to keep a chart showing methods of stain removal and suitable fabrics to use them on in the kitchen.

If these treatments do not work you will need to send clothes to the dry cleaner or use a dry cleaning machine.

Activity

Using the machine can save you a lot of money. Find out how much it would cost to dry clean the following in a dry cleaning machine and at the cleaners:

1 lady's skirt
2 pairs men's trousers
1 man's jacket
1 lady's dress
1 child's coat

SEE ALSO

Labelling for information about dry cleaning agents.

Ventilation

Ventilation means changing the stale air in a room for fresh.
Figure 108 shows some different ways of ventilating a room.

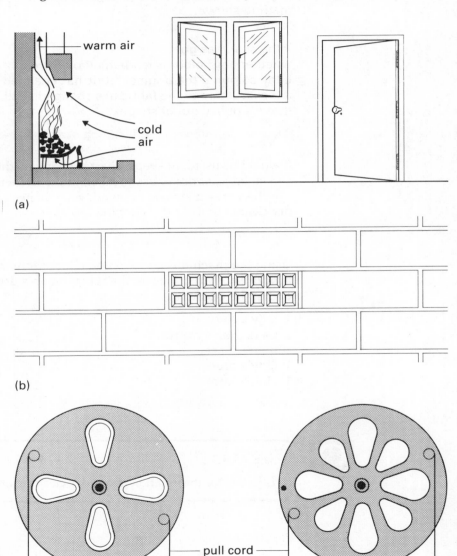

Figure 108
Ventilation. (part)
(a) Ventilating a room
   with a coal fire.
(b) Air brick.
(c) Cooper's disc.

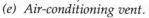

Figure 108
Ventilation. (continued)
(d) Extractor fan.
(e) Air-conditioning vent.

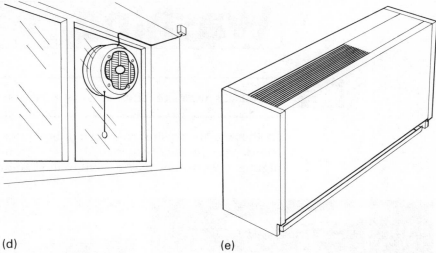

(d)   (e)

Figure 108a shows a coal fire. Hot air rises up the chimney and cold air is drawn from the room to replace it. This may make a room feel draughty. Doors and windows can also provide ventilation. Small top-opening windows cause less of a draught.

Figure 108b shows air bricks set high in the outside wall of a room which does not have a fireplace.

Figure 108c shows Cooper's disc. This is fitted in a window and may be in the open or closed position. It may also be fitted to a cooker hood.

Figure 108d shows an extractor fan. This is fitted into a window. It works electrically and is expensive to install and can be noisy. It draws stale air and cooking smells out of a room.

Figure 108e shows an air-conditioning vent. This is a complete system controlling the temperature and humidity (moisture content) of the air circulated round a building.

Activity

Which do you think would be suitable for:

a kitchen
bedroom   room with a gas fire
an office block   a bathroom?

It is important not to make a home so draught-proof that there is no ventilation, especially if there are gas appliances. There are sometimes reports in the newspapers of people who have died while asleep from a build-up of fumes from a gas appliance.

What other reasons are there for providing good ventilation?

Washing

 Collect samples of different types of fabrics.

Clothes may be washed in a bowl of hot water in the sink, at the launderette, in one of the many types of washing machine available (figures 109), or they may be sent to the laundry.

(a)

(b)

Figure 109   (part)
(a) Single-tub washing machine.

(b) Fully automatic washing machine.

Figure 109   (continued)
(c) Twin-tub
*   washing machine*

The way you choose which method is suitable for you may depend on:

money
amount of washing
time available for washing.

Home washing has been made easier by the use of the International Textile Care Codes, which can be found on most clothes and furnishings. (See pages 110 and 111.)

When washing, sort clothes into piles according to their colour group and labels. If you are using an automatic washing machine set it for the process shown on the label. If you are using a twin- or single-tub follow the instructions for machine wash.

Washing powders will also have information about the wash codes. All items with the same temperature can safely be washed together as long as they are colour-fast.

Activity

Try carrying out a weekly wash at the launderette and by washing machine.

Compare the cost, time taken, and results.

What do you think are the advantages and disadvantages of each?

Which washing powder should you choose?

Detergents are used to detach dirt from clothes, dissolve grease, and prevent dirt from being redeposited on clothes.

There are seven different types of detergent you could use for washing clothes.

1) Synthetic detergents *e.g.* Daz

These do not contain any soap. They can be used for washing by hand or machine (except for fully automatics). They produce a good lather even in hard water and are easy to rinse away.

2) Soap powders *e.g.* Persil

These are made from animal or vegetable fats. They are good for washing by hand or machine but may produce a scum in hard water areas.

3) Biological (enzyme) detergents *e.g.* Radiant

These are synthetic (man-made) detergents which contain enzymes which break down protein stains such as blood, milk, and egg. They are useful for soaking stains before washing and work best at hand-hot temperatures (not above 60 °C). Some people have an allergic reaction to enzyme detergents. They develop skin rashes which may occur not only when the detergent is being used, but when clothes are worn after washing. Using rubber gloves will help in avoiding skin contact, but if rashes persist a change of washing powder may be necessary.

4) Low-lather detergents *e.g.* Bold, Persil Automatic

These are specially made to use in front-loading automatic washing machines. They do not make as much foam, as this could stop the washing machine from working properly.

5) Low-temperature detergents

These detergents have been developed specially to work when the water is at a lower temperature. Some washing machines have an economy wash cycle to use with these. They are a way of saving money spent on fuel for heating water.

6) Grease-solvent washing powders *e.g.* Drive

These are specially for removing greasy or fatty marks and stains from clothes and furnishings.

7) **Light-duty detergents** *e.g.* Stergene

These are suitable for hand-washing delicate items such as woollens. They are easy to rinse away and leave clothes feeling soft.

Activity

Most detergents can be bought in a range of sizes. Take one detergent and find out how much it costs for each size. Which is the cheapest size per unit weight to buy? (A calculator or a spreadsheet program for the computer will help with this.)

Fabric conditioners

These are added to the rinsing water to make clothes feel softer, to add body, and to reduce static electricity (this makes clothes cling, and also attracts dirt). They give a soft, fluffy feel, particularly to towels and woollens.

Activity

Stain some of the fabrics you have collected in the same way, for example with mud or food. Wash in each of the seven detergents listed, following the instructions on the pack. Make a chart to show which detergent gave the best results with each fabric and present your findings to the rest of the group.

SEE ALSO

Stain removal for how to remove stains from fabric.
Labelling for more about the International Textile Care Codes.

Free leaflets about care labels are available from The International Textile Consultative Council, care of the Clothing and Footwear Institute (address on page 180).

Waste disposal

Every household produces waste daily. This may be liquid waste from toilets, sinks, and rainwater, or solid waste such as tins, bottles, packets, and food waste. The local authority is responsible for disposing of this waste by providing refuse collections, and mains drains and sewers, and emptying septic tanks; but we are all responsible for making sure that our waste is ready for collection in a way that is clean and safe. If this is not done correctly it may become smelly and encourage flies and rats and disease-carrying bacteria.

Getting rid of liquid waste

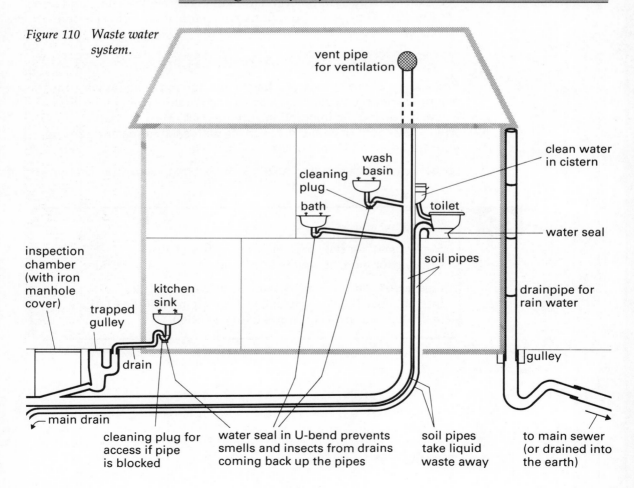

Figure 110 Waste water system.

vent pipe for ventilation

cleaning plug

wash basin

bath

toilet

clean water in cistern

water seal

soil pipes

inspection chamber (with iron manhole cover)

trapped gulley

kitchen sink

drainpipe for rain water

gulley

drain

main drain

cleaning plug for access if pipe is blocked

water seal in U-bend prevents smells and insects from drains coming back up the pipes

soil pipes take liquid waste away

to main sewer (or drained into the earth)

Figure 110 shows how liquid waste is disposed of when it leaves a house.

See if you can find the things in figure 110 in your own home, and draw your own plan.

When the liquid waste has left a house it passes into the sewers and on to the sewage works (figure 111).

Figure 111 Sewage treatment works.

To make it harmless the bacteria in it have to be killed off. This is done by using other bacteria and by the action of air. The solid sludge sinks to the bottom and separates from the liquid. The sludge is removed and treated with more bacteria. It is then rotted and sold for fertilizer (it is "recycled"). When the liquid is safe it is allowed to flow back into the rivers.

Cesspits and septic tanks

Some homes in country areas cannot be connected to mains drainage. They have to have a septic tank or cesspit.

Septic tanks
These are two dug-out areas below ground level. The sewage drains into the first and is broken down into a more liquid form. The sludge sinks to the bottom and is removed by the council. The liquid passes into the second area where it becomes harmless and drains into the soil.

Cesspits
A cesspit is a well sealed dug-out area below the ground; the sewage drains into this. When it is full it is emptied by the council, who fit a suction hose and drain it into a covered cart and take it to the sewage works for treatment.

Keeping the toilet clean

The toilet can contain millions of bacteria, so it is important to keep it clean and fresh-smelling. There is a wide range of cleaners to choose from in most shops.

Activities

What do you really want a toilet cleaner to do? You should be able to think of at least three things.
   List a range of items you can buy for the toilet.
   Which of these do you think is the strongest cleaner?
   Which would you use:

For cleaning the toilet bowl?
For cleaning the toilet seat, handle of the cistern, and door knobs?
To keep the toilet smelling nice?

Find out the names and prices of the cleaners available in a shop near you. How would you choose between them?
   Are you getting anything more for your money if you pay more?

DO NOT mix toilet cleaners. If you use bleach together with other toilet cleaners poisonous fumes can be given off, so choose one cleaner and stick to that.

Figure 112

Care is needed when storing all cleaners when there are young children in the house. What is dangerous in figure 112? How could you improve things?

Remember

*To clean the toilet every day (if you do not have much time for cleaning this is the one job you should always do – much more important than dusting).

*To keep a brush for cleaning the toilet bowl in a little disinfectant in a special holder and use it only for that purpose.

*To keep all cloths used in the toilet just for this purpose.

*To keep the window open. It's cheaper than buying air fresheners!

Keeping sinks and basins clean

Activity

There are also many cleaners for sinks and basins. What would you expect them to do?

Which of the cleaners in figure 113 would you use for:

a stainless steel sink
a vitreous enamel sink
a plastic bath
a porcelain basin?

Would it be possible to have just one cleaner for all the sinks or basins in your home?

Figure 113

Remember

*To clean sinks and basins every day to stop dirt building up.

*To wash down with hot soapy water after use and run fresh water the U-bend.

Blocked sinks

If the water in the sink will not run away, or if it runs away very slowly, it may have become blocked with bits of food, fat, or soap.

1) Try putting soda crystals in the sink and pouring boiling water over. This will usually clear it.
OR
2) If this doesn't work, use a plunger and press up and down (figure 114).
OR
3) If neither of these work call a plumber.

Figure 114   Clearing a blocked sink.

Getting rid of solid waste

Solid rubbish goes into the dustbin and is collected by the council. We pay for this service in the rates.

Activity/Discussion

Dustbins can be of several types. Match up the bins in figure 115 with the description(s) which you think will fit.

Light in weight	Quiet
Noisy	Not suitable for hot ashes
Not suitable for glass	Easily damaged
Heavy	

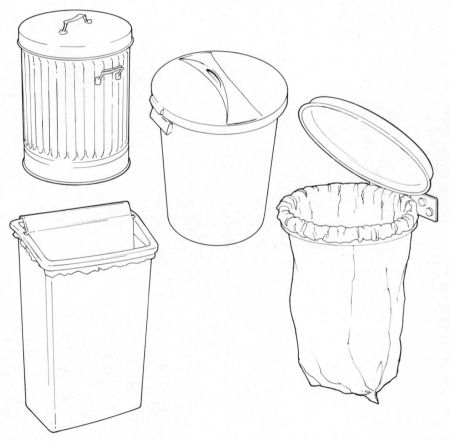

Figure 115

Which type of dustbin do you think is best and why?

Look at figure 116. What is happening in each drawing?
How could these problems be avoided?

Figure 116   (part)

Figure 116   (continued)   A great deal of the waste we throw away every day is packaging (figure 117).

Figure 117   Packaging waste.

Why do you think packaging is necessary? Could we cut down on this type of waste?

Recycling

In some areas waste is recycled (processed in some way and used again). What do you think could be done with the waste in figure 118?

Figure 118

Keeping the dustbin clean

Dustbins should be rinsed out regularly with disinfectant. If you don't have bin liners use newspaper to line the bin. Dustbin powder improves the smell.

Pedal bins

We often put our rubbish into a smaller bin indoors before putting it in the dustbin. Pedal bins should be lined otherwise they will become smelly. You can buy pedal bin liners (large plastic bags) for this, or use newspaper or plastic bags from shopping. Pedal bins should be emptied daily and washed out before lining again.

What happens to the waste after collection?

Once the rubbish from a house has been collected by the dustman it may end up in various places.

Some rubbish is dumped in the sea, far enough out to prevent it washing back onto beaches.

Some rubbish ends up on rubbish dumps (figure 119).

These are areas well away from houses where the rubbish is tipped. Sometimes it is covered with earth, or burnt.

Rubbish dumps look awful, smell, and attract rats and flies. The rubbish often blows around the nearby area.

Figure 119

Figure 120   Waste disposal plant in West Drayton, Greater London.

The most hygienic way of getting rid of rubbish is in a refuse disposal plant (figure 120).

In a refuse disposal plant rubbish which can be re-used is sorted out: for example tins are removed with magnets, plastic and paper is sold for use as fuel for industry. Rubbish which cannot be burned, like broken china, is used for filling in land. Rubbish which cannot be used is burned and the ashes sold for fertiliser. The money from selling the reuseable rubbish helps to pay for the refuse disposal plant, which is expensive to run.

Discussion

Which parts of the country are likely to have each of the types of rubbish disposal mentioned above?

Other ways of disposing of rubbish

Chutes

Large blocks of flats sometimes have a large central chute with an opening in or near each kitchen. The rubbish goes down this chute and into large bins which are emptied by the council.

Rubbish should be wrapped to stop the chute getting smelly.

Figure 121   Waste disposal unit.

Waste disposal units

A waste disposal unit (figure 121) fits under the sink and grinds waste into a pulp which can be rinsed away. They are hygienic, but expensive to buy and fit.

Which of these could not be put down the waste disposal unit:

food waste
cans
string
paper waste, *e.g.* cartons
cloth?

Choose a waste disposal unit which will not work without a guard in place, if you have young children in the house. The on/off switch should also be well out of their reach.

SEE ALSO

Rates for more about how we pay for getting rid of our waste.

Try to arrange a visit to your local sewage works.

List of Addresses

Advertising Standards
    Authority (ASA),
2–16 Torrington Place,
London,
W1E 7HN.

Advisory Unit for Computer-
    Based Education (AUCBE),
Endymion Road,
Hatfield,
Hertfordshire,
AL10 8AU.

Banking Information Service,
10 Lombard Street.
London,
EC3V 9AT.

Beebugsoft,
P.O. Box 50,
St Albans,
Hertfordshire.

British Gas,
326 High Holborn,
London,
WC1V 7PT.

British Gas Education Service,
P.O. Box 46,
Hounslow,
Middlesex,
TW4 6NF.

British Standards Institution
    (BSI)
2 Park Street,
London,
W1A 2BS.

BSI Sales Department,
Linford Wood,
Milton Keynes,
MK14 6LE.

Cambridge University Press,
The Edinburgh Building,
Shaftesbury Road,
Cambridge,
CD2 2RU.

Clothing and Footwear Institute,
71 Brushfield Street,
London,
E1 6AA.

Concord Films Council Ltd,
201 Felixstowe Road,
Ipswich,
Suffolk,
IP3 9BJ.

Consumers' Association,
14 Buckingham Street
London WC2N 6DS.

Design Centre,
28 Haymarket,
London,
SW1.

Electricity Council,
30 Millbank,
London,
SWIP 4RD.

Energy Efficiency Office,
Room 1312,
Thames House South,
Millbank,
London,
SWIP 4QJ.

Longman Micro Software,
62 Hallfield Road,
Layerthorpe,
York,
YO3 7XQ.

Office of Fair Trading,
Field House,
15–25 Breams Buildings,
London,
EC4A 1PR.

RML,
P.O. Box 75,
Mill Street,
Oxford,
OX2 OBW.

Welsh Consumer Council,
Oxford House,
Hills Street,
Cardiff,
CF1 2DR.

Index